I0155578

They Devour in Silence

ii

They Devour in Silence
Tales from an Exorcist in Chicago

By Phil Mendoza & Patricia K. Reyes

Copyright © 2023 Phil Mendoza and Patricia K. Reyes
All rights reserved.
ISBN-13: 979-8-218-19745-2

Acknowledgements

First of all, I'd like to thank Mercury, Kali, Venus, Jupiter, Hecate, and Diana for their patience and guidance. Additional gratitude goes to Ptah, Ra Horakhty, and Ganesha, for their continued inspiration and abundant insight. I also want to thank Raphael, Michael, Gabriel, Auriel, Sandalphon, Metatron, and the choirs of angels for their assistance on this oftentimes grueling, but rewarding path.

A huge thank you also goes to my writer and friend, Patricia; thank you for enduring this journey alongside me. Thank you Alyssa and Joe for somehow accepting our science experiment/reality home and family. Thanks to Sarah Greyson for the creation of this book cover, and to the Golden Dawn Collegium, for all of their support and fellowship. To all, love and bright blessings.

Above all, thank you God for the challenges which promote growth, exploration, and love.

Table of Contents

"Teach me (O Creator of all things) to have correct knowledge and understanding, for your wisdom is all that I desire. Speak your word in my ear (O Creator of all things) and set your wisdom in my heart."

- Dr. John Dee

Preface

I n an increasingly secular world, where we are bombarded on a daily basis with the mundane concerns of modern life, it is easy to shrug aside the unseen forces in our lives. Family, friends, and career tend to take center stage in our lives; and rightfully so. However, our ignorance of the invisible realms does not render them any less potent or impactful on our material reality.

Over the last decade, reports of possession and spiritual oppression to the Vatican have increased exponentially. In response to this demand, the Catholic church has expanded its training, to prepare more and more parishioners to become full-fledged exorcists. Unfortunately, their efforts have been insufficient in treating the sheer volume of reports.

The stringent criteria that are required in order to qualify for a Catholic exorcism precludes the vast majority of cases, and reports have come in from individuals of all belief systems. A significant level of proof is required for this service, which is often very difficult to capture or quantify in a way that will provide any sort of objective evidence for the oppression. It is also important to note that the so-called 'demonic' oppressions account for a mere fraction of the phenomena that is at play here.

Spiritual disturbances are a cross-cultural phenomenon, and not all unseen influences are rooted in the Christian paradigm. Every belief system has its own pantheon of entities, which tend to respond best to practices within their own paradigmatic system. Even more compelling, is the fact that the target's belief, or lack thereof, has little to no bearing on whether or not they are attacked. While the ontological implications of this convoluted mass of phenomena are beyond the scope of this book, it is imperative to be aware that no one is immune to spiritual oppression.

On top of all of this, lies a final component which further complicates these already murky waters, and that is the dramatic rise of mental illness in our society. Not all reported cases are spiritual in nature, and it takes a high level of caution and discernment to determine whether a person is in need of an exorcism, or just needs to seek psychological help. And, as is often the case, both mental illness and spiritual oppression have a role to play in what a person is experiencing.

Handling these types of situations takes not only a great deal of skill and esoteric knowledge, but also a high degree of empathy, compassion, and humility. Any practitioner who decides to pursue this path should always keep their client's wellbeing at the forefront of their mind. Any expectations of monetary rewards or accolades completely misses the purpose of doing this kind of work. In fact, for the first ten years of doing this, I did not require any compensation.

The only reason that I ever made the difficult decision to implement a sliding scale fee, was because my efforts were often devalued by my clients, and I needed them to treat the situation with the gravity that it deserved. For my services to truly do what they are meant to, my clients need to share my commitment to their healing process. I have a family and a full-time career; what I do, I do because I feel a calling from deep within my soul to do it. This work is a labor of love, because I know firsthand what it is like to be haunted and oppressed by unseen forces.

My first supernatural experience occurred when I was about 12 years old. My family had just moved in to an old, two-story home on the outskirts of Chicago. While the house was relatively small, it was larger than what my family had been used to by that point, and there had been a great deal of excitement in the air. Unfortunately, from the moment I walked through that front door, I wanted to leave.

No matter what part of the house I was in, it felt like I was being watched. Moving through the home felt oddly like I was invading someone else's space, and I always had the distinct impression that I was not alone there, even when the rest of the family was gone. Nowhere in that house felt safe to me, and I avoided being alone as much as possible when I was there. This was fairly easy to do, as there were seven of us squeezed into that modest, suburban house. However, at night, this was a very different story.

Shortly after we'd moved in, I would get dragged from my bed on a near-nightly basis. The first time it happened, and I'd woken up on the floor in front of my closet, I assumed I'd been sleepwalking. However, as time went on, and I'd wake to find my hands desperately clutching the carpet, my fingernails red and bloodied, I began to realize that something more sinister had been taking place.

The long days stretched into longer nights, as time dragged on, and sleep eluded me. I'd become increasingly paranoid. The few times I'd allowed myself to disclose what I'd been experiencing at night, I was told I had an overactive imagination, and that it had been nothing more than a bad dream. For a short time, I even convinced myself that that was true. That was when my situation began to get worse.

In my small, second-story bedroom, was one ancient, dusty window. Even though the glass was scratched and dingy, that window had also been a source of comfort in my dark nights, as it had allowed a bit of moonlight to filter in. As my ill fortune would have it, we soon discovered that the section of the wall near my bedroom window was beginning to rot. The especially humid summer we'd been having was expediting that process.

To make the situation worse, the rotting wood had created an opening on the exterior portion of the wall, and some bees had moved into that cavity and created a hive. Hoping to avoid any potential incidents with our insectoid tenants, my father had then decided to board off that whole section of wall; including my bedroom window. After that, my nights got much darker; both literally and figuratively.

Once I flipped the light switch, my bedroom was enveloped in an unending darkness. My heart was pounding, and my palms were sweating, as I shut my lids tightly, trying desperately to fall sleep. Still, even in that close silence, I could feel eyes on me. A palpable presence hung in the room. When I could no longer keep my eyes closed, I stole a peek at the blackened space where my bedroom used to be. What I saw made my hair stand on end.

A faint glow of light, in the shape of a human figure, hung in the air near the side of my bed. My first impulse had been to look away, horrified at the possibility that I was being presented with. Once I'd eventually summoned the courage to look squarely at my visitor, I saw what appeared to be a male figure, dressed in Renaissance-era garb, standing near my bed, with his gaze fixed firmly on me.

This became a near-nightly occurrence, and sleep would continue to elude me. I quickly learned not to share my experiences with others, as I was always met with pity and judgment, at best. Even the local clergy could do nothing to help me rid myself of this unwanted phenomenon. Needless to say, this had lit a fire under me to get a job, and move out of that house as quickly as possible.

Years later, once I'd finally achieved my independence, I was having a gathering at my apartment. My girlfriend at the time had decided to sleep over, and we'd gone to bed late, though uneventfully. Well into the wee, dark hours of the morning, my girlfriend had rolled over and woken up. Once she'd noticed that I was not lying in bed next to her, she looked over to see me sitting up straight at the foot of the bed, facing the bedroom door. When she'd crawled over to me to see what was wrong, she'd noticed that I was talking, as if to some invisible audience, though I was still clearly asleep. She'd reasoned that I must be talking in my sleep, and gently shook my shoulder and told me to come back to bed.

Instantly, as if in response, a figure materialized through the door and entered the room. Panicked, my girlfriend let out a terrified cry, which pulled me quickly out of my sleep state. Once I'd consoled her enough to explain what had happened, she described for me, in stunning detail, the exact same Renaissance figure that had haunted my bedroom as a child. The shock of that confirmation struck me in the chest like a ton of bricks; whatever that thing was, it was very real, and it had followed me into my new home.

The trauma of those early experiences, coupled with the validation of that fateful night, planted a resolve in me. I was determined to learn how to banish that thing from my life, and to use that knowledge to help others who were similarly tormented. I never wanted anyone to feel the way that I had felt back then; helpless, confused, and alone.

That search inevitably led me to join a variety of esoteric occult orders, where I would gain the tools to take charge of my own aura, or sphere of sensation. One such tool was using the methods of Solomonic magick, in order to divine the name of the oppressing entity, summon it, and banish it. This is in stark contrast to the methods of a traditional Catholic exorcism, where the priest is metaphorically hammering away at the demon. Using the methods of Solomonic magick, I am not necessarily ousting the entity itself; I am simply dissolving the hold it has on its host, and redistributing and balancing the energy of that entity. In addition to these methods, I have also borrowed much of my practice from my fellow magickians in the Golden Dawn Collegium Spiritus Sancti. My magickal brothers and sisters have proved an invaluable resource in this field of practice, for both their moral support and their practical expertise.

Similarly, I owe a great debt of gratitude to the writings of esoteric scholar Lon Milo DuQuette; namely his work in *My Life with the Spirits* and *Homemade Magick*. His candor and wisdom have been indispensable in my own work. I've also employed the methods outlined in Poke Runyon's *Dark Mirror Magick*. I frequently make use of his system in doing my divinations. Finally, abundant thanks go to Josephine McCarthy and her bodies of work; *The Exorcist's Handbook*, in particular. Her writings on the occult exorcism have proved invaluable to me.

I am always filled with gratitude when I can truly help someone, and many of my clients have become good friends of mine. Still others prefer to sever contact with me, as my very presence is a grim reminder of their recent torment. Regardless, I always respect my clients' decisions and rights to privacy. As such, the names and some of the locations of my clients have been changed for the stories in this book, to respect their anonymity and personal lives.

This work is not for the faint of heart, and I do not recommend it for the casual practitioner. These entities have a way of bleeding into your life, even long after your work with the client has concluded. It is not to be taken lightly, and it will absolutely change your life as you know it now. If you do feel truly called to embark on a journey such as this, it is imperative that you have a strong support system, a regular spiritual practice, and a pristine sphere of sensation.

It is the nature of all wayward spirits to try and regain their foothold in the material world, with all the sensations and emotions that accompany a physical existence. To avoid becoming sustenance for starving, lower energies, we must strive to find balance and resolve in our daily lives; lest they consume and devour even our best of intentions.

Case Study 1: Jessica

The gentle rays of golden sunlight pierced the stained-glass window by my fireplace, painting the living room floor in undulating streams of red, purple, and orange. I sat quietly at my desk, reveling in the early morning silence; it would be hours before teenage footsteps were heard on the stairs and lawn mowers across the block roared to life. Softening my awareness, a technique I'd learned long ago, I slipped into a meditative state.

Minutes swam by; or maybe they were hours? It was hard to know for sure from within that liminal state; each moment dissolved into the next, in an unending series of instants.

As I eventually began to ground myself back into my body, a familiar vibration stirred on the periphery of my consciousness. Slowly, deliberately opening my eyes, I spied my phone vibrating jarringly on the desk in front of me.

Still a bit disoriented from my meditation, I had only a moment to glance at the name on the Caller ID before the call was redirected to voicemail.

Jessica? Jessica Evans?

Though she was a good friend, who I'd met while doing some work at the local occult bookstore, I hadn't seen or spoken to her in months. Another quick glance at my phone confirmed the time: 6:45am. I couldn't imagine why she'd be calling quite that early; and on a Sunday no less.

I was still pondering this, when the phone began vibrating once more, in a persistent, rhythmic buzz. The screen glowed in gold pixelated letters: Jessica Evans.

In one fluid motion, I swiped the phone and tapped the green Answer button.

"Hey Jessica, what's up?" I muttered, attempting in vain to sound more awake than I felt.

"Hey Phil," the phone chirped into my ear. Her voice sounded thin, and ached with exhaustion. "I think there's something weird going on at my mom's house."

It took me a moment to ascertain the subtle meaning behind Jessica's words. *Something weird going on.* Finally, it clicked.

"Ok," I said. "Tell me what's happening." Hesitant at first, Jessica began to explain, and before long, the story began to unfold.

Jessica and her mother had lived in their home for nearly a decade. It was a modest, well-kept rental property, in a quiet suburban neighborhood. Still a young adult in her early 20's, Jessica was living with her mother at the time. Although they'd lived there for years, only recently had the strange series of events began to occur.

As she began describing the phenomena she'd been experiencing, her voice shook, sounding strained and fragile. It was clear that Jessica was uncomfortably aware of how bizarre it all sounded, and very guarded about making such outrageous claims out loud. She had repeatedly been hearing strange noises and movement throughout the house, with no discernible origin. According to her, the noises sounded as if someone was walking around on their floor, even though she knew full well that she was the only person home. There were also the strange, darting shadows that seemed to elude her investigations, coupled with random foul odors and inexplicable cold spots in various areas around the property.

"Who else has been experiencing these things?" I asked.

There was silence, followed by the sound of an exasperated, weary sigh.

"No one," she muttered softly. "It's just me."

I could sense the desperation in her voice and I was intimately familiar with that feeling. I knew all too well what it was like to experience terrifying supernatural phenomena, and to be shunned or ostracized when you decide to share your story with others. This hadn't been an easy call for her to make. It also wasn't the type of call I'd become accustomed to receiving just yet.

I'd been a practicing member of the Order of the Golden Dawn for well over a decade, and I'd had extensive experience working with non-corporeal entities, but I still had a lot to learn. At this point, I hadn't done much banishing or spirit-removal work in the public arena. I wanted very much to help her out, but I was unsure where to begin.

"What's changed in the home recently?" I began, figuring that was as good a place to start as any. "Have you brought in any new antiques? Second-hand clothing from a thrift store? Anything like that?"

As we worked our way through my mental checklist, I became increasingly disheartened. We couldn't seem to identify any specific source for the developing phenomena. Uncertain of how to proceed, I informed her that I'd make some notes about what she'd told me, and get back to her when I had a solid plan of action.

This seemed to satisfy her for the time being. However, I had the sneaking suspicion that these recent events were just the tip of the iceberg; whatever was behind this mayhem was just getting started.

"And listen, Jess," I interjected quickly, before disconnecting the call. "Let me know as soon as possible if these things start to escalate."

Very soon, they did.

—

Before long, I was receiving phone calls and texts from Jessica on an almost daily basis. The activity was intensifying exponentially, and she was feeling more and more isolated, as she continued to be the only person experiencing the peculiar disturbances.

Not only were the previous phenomena still occurring, but now the mysterious shadows were becoming bolder. At all times of the day or night, she was seeing short, humanoid, shadowy figures, about 2-3 feet tall, skulking around the house. However, the most disconcerting of these new developments was when she had gotten pinned down on her bed, seemingly by the curtains of her bedroom window.

She'd reported being awoken by a massive weight on her chest, and opened her eyes to see the draperies pressing down around her. As she struggled to free herself, she noted that it was like trying to fight off a cascading waterfall; there was no identifiable source behind the strength or the form of what was oppressing her, and it felt like it was coming at her from every angle.

Quickly becoming concerned for my friend's safety, I finally decided to consult my fellow Order members for advice on how best to proceed. After a handful of discussions and divinations, we compiled a list of rituals and prayers to use. Much to my surprise, they seemed far more confident in my abilities to accomplish the task than I felt was warranted. Their final, optimistic advice was simply: "Go do what you do and kick some ass!"

As soon as I got home, I called Jessica.

"I'm going to need a few hours alone in the house to do some work," I told her. "I'll be bringing some things with me; incense, a set of prayers, that kind of stuff."

"Oh," she responded, sounding faintly surprised. "Let me talk to my mom and see when she might be out of the house for a few hours, and I'll get back to you."

"Just so you know," I informed her, "it's only going to get worse, the longer we wait."

What followed, over the next few weeks, was an unending back and forth, trying to balance both our schedules and find a time that worked. I was working long hours at the time, so finding a suitable day where both I was available and her mother happened to be out of the house, was becoming increasingly difficult.

It was 4am on a stuffy morning in August when I received her panicked phone call.

"It attacked my boyfriend!" she sobbed, her voice thick with fear. In the middle of the night, something had pinned her boyfriend down on the bed, and had begun swiveling his head back and forth, side to side, in rapid succession. Justin, a muscular young man in his 20's, who I'd only met once, was well over six feet tall, and roughly 200 pounds. Holding him down would have been no small feat for anyone, let alone a disembodied spirit. Worried that the violent, jerking motions might injure him, Jessica had straddled his chest, choking back sobs as she attempted to hold his head safely in place.

Justin, caught up in this rude awakening, had naturally assumed that she was the one flipping his head back and forth.

"What the hell are you doing?!" he'd screeched in confusion, still unable to free himself.

"I'm trying to stop it before it hurts you!" she'd screamed back at him.

Eventually, the force had relinquished its hold, and Justin had quickly fled the scene, but the damage had already been done. Although he had purportedly believed her claims, that something invisible was the culprit and that she'd only been trying to stop it, the seeds of doubt had been planted. This event had taken its toll on both of them; not just a physical one, but an emotional one as well. It was clear to me that time was running out.

5

The next morning, I gathered my tools, and made the half-hour trip to Jessica's house.

—

Cleverly, Jessica had managed to lure her mother out of the house that day with an impromptu gift certificate to a day spa. As I pulled into the driveway, Jessica was leaning against her car waiting for me, tapping away at her phone, her tawny dreadlocks hanging thick like vines around her slender face. She couldn't have weighed more than 90 pounds, and barely stood at 5 feet tall. The thought of her being able to overpower Justin, looking at her now, was laughably absurd. I chuckled inwardly at the mental image, and steeled myself for what I knew awaited me inside.

As I gathered my tools and stepped out of the car, I realized I'd never been to her home before. The way she'd described it during our many phone calls, I'd pictured it as an unassuming, single story family home. However, the property I was at now clearly had an upper level.

"I didn't know you guys had a second floor," I mentioned casually. "What's up there?"

"Oh, that's not ours," she said, glancing up from her phone. "It's a separate living space, I dunno who our landlord rented it out to. Haven't seen anyone coming or going in a while."

Shrugging it off for the moment, I locked my car, and headed towards the front door. Jessica slipped her phone into the pocket of her tattered jeans and walked over to meet me.

"Do you need anything else before I leave?" she asked, eyes darting nervously between the bag in my hands and the front door looming ahead.

"Nope. Just go do something fun and try not to dwell too much on what's going on. I'll call you when I'm finished and ready for you to come back."

With a brief nod, she turned on her heels and quickly got in her car and left.

As I crossed the threshold, pulling the door shut behind me, my senses were assaulted with a smell that was at once both chemical and floral; scented candles, and a lot of them. None were lit at the moment, but it was clear by the subtle scent of smoke that they had been recently snuffed. *Someone was trying to mask an odor*, came my first thought.

Taking a quick look around, I decided that the most thorough route would be to start at the back bedroom and work my way through the rest of the house. Once the incense was lit, and the pages of sanctifying prayers were in order, I began the cleansing.

The sweet, intoxicating aroma of frankincense and myrrh filled the room, as my chants and prayers echoed faintly. In a few quick minutes, her mother's bedroom was finished. I swung the censer as I made my way down the short hallway and into the living room. The overstuffed, slightly faded sofa looked strangely alluring; I hadn't gotten much sleep the night before. Suddenly, I felt extremely drowsy, and for the briefest of moments I contemplated taking a quick nap, right then and there.

No, I thought, shaking my head as if to symbolically clear it. Though the banishing had been uneventful so far, the impulse felt forced; as if it had come, not from my own mind, but from something outside of it, attempting to catch me off guard. Emboldened by this realization, I pressed forward.

Before long, I'd completed the banishing in the living room, and began making my way towards the front of the house. They had an open-concept kitchen, connecting seamlessly with a cozy dining area, which was furnished with a square dining table and four wooden chairs. By this time, I'd begun noticing a distinct change in the energy of the house.

With each step I took, the air around me became thicker and thicker, until it felt like I was trudging through a raging river, fighting against an unforgiving current. Whatever was infesting this home clearly did not want me to be there. Even then, as new as I was to this sort of work, I took that as a solemn warning.

Proceed with caution, I thought, taking one more determined step towards the kitchen. Instantly, all the ambient noises around me went dead silent, and the hair on the back of my neck stood straight up. It wasn't just the sounds of the house that had ceased; it was as if time itself had stopped for a brief moment, in an infinitesimal void of nothingness. This thing was about to make its move.

CRACK.

Before I knew what had happened, an invisible force struck me directly in the chest, with so much momentum that it knocked me back against the opposite wall. I crumpled to the ground like a discarded ragdoll, my incense and stack of papers fluttering to the floor around me. It felt as if someone had struck me in the solar plexus with a sledgehammer, as though I were one of those 'Test Your Strength' machines at a county fair.

My lungs heaved and strained, trying desperately to regain the air that had been thoroughly bludgeoned out of them. I lay on the floor in a daze, my left leg dangling helplessly from an overturned chair nearby. Concentrating on the sound of my ragged breathing, I attempted to regain my focus. Though my chest had taken the full weight of the assault, I was certain I'd hit my head also, and for a brief moment I was lost in a disorienting fog.

GET UP, commanded a voice in my head. *GET UP NOW OR THIS THING IS GOING TO KILL YOU.*

The pain radiating from the impact made every movement a struggle. After a handful of attempts, I was able to roll over onto my stomach and pull myself up off the floor. With all the gracefulness of a drunken sailor, I gathered up my scattered tools. Planting both feet squarely on the ground, I whispered a quick prayer for fortitude, and continued with the banishing ritual.

I could feel the entity's rage; the walls vibrated with it. Every word was a battlefield, as I fought to breathe through the pain in my chest. The dense, surging energy was like a lead curtain, and I could only take shallow, wheezing gasps, still injured from the violent assault. It took what felt like an eternity to complete the litany, and more than once I was convinced that I would not make it out of that house alive.

Finally, as I neared the final calls of the banishing ritual, the energy dissipated as quickly as it had condensed. Without skipping a beat, I began the final prayers in earnest, and all around me the house relaxed, as though breathing a sigh of relief.

In an effort to be as thorough as possible, I completed the working in the back bedroom as well, though intuitively I knew that whatever had been here was gone now.

But, I thought, *where the hell did this thing come from?*

It made me slightly uncomfortable that we still hadn't identified the source of this supernatural melodrama. As I packed away my tools and straightened up some furniture that had been knocked over during the conflict, I brainstormed about what could have caused this type of dangerous oppression. Just before I hit the Send button on the text message I'd composed, to let Jessica know that it was now safe to come home, a flash of light caught my eye: it was the reflection of sunlight, bouncing off of a chandelier, which was suspended over the dining room table. I hadn't noticed that when I'd first entered the room. That was when it dawned on me.

Maybe the activity had originated from the living space on the second floor? It was the only area of the building that I hadn't been given access to, and Jessica seemed to know very little about what went on up there. I made a mental note to ask her more about that when she got back, and hit Send.

—

A week later, Jessica called to let me know that she'd found out what the situation upstairs was. Apparently, for the last few years, their landlord had been renting out the top floor to various members of a local substance abuse clinic, for those who could only pay by the night.

9

It had been a high traffic area for people with severe trauma and mental health issues. In fact, there had been multiple suicides and overdoses on the floor above. Once she'd informed me of this, I finally realized what the source of the phenomena was.

The sheer rage and despair that accompanies acute mental health problems calls in all manner of destructive entities. That, coupled with a string of suicides, had created a dark vortex of energy, lighting a beacon for restless beings who longed to have physical agency once more. Once that murky, stagnant energy had reached critical mass, it could no longer be contained on the floor above, and it had begun seeping into the living space below, where it found fresh new victims to feed on. Their home had become a hunting ground for all those disembodied spirits who were bitter and starving for a way to press themselves into the material world. I also soon discovered that whatever force had struck me down had indeed managed to fracture my sternum.

Upon viewing my x-rays, the doctor had asked me, in all seriousness, if I'd been in a very bad car accident. I'd fought against the urge to laugh in that moment, because in a way, that was kind of what it had felt like. In an attempt to keep the bitter smirk off of my face, I'd shaken my head in response.

"No, nothing like that," I'd said, waving my hand dismissively. "Something happened, but I'm not really ready to talk about it right now."

He'd looked at me sideways, suspiciously, as if he'd been convinced that I was a member of some kind of underground fight club. Shrugging it off, he'd set my chart down and nodded, and hadn't pressed me further.

I was beyond relieved that this ordeal was over, and to date, Jessica has reported no further activity in her home. I had completed my work, but the fracture in my chest remains as a grim reminder of what transpired, and the dangers of allowing the darker angels of our nature to take over.

Case Study 2: Andrew

The autumnal trees that flew past the window of my Chevy pickup truck were but a fiery orange blur as I sped along the highway. I'd just wrapped up a particularly challenging project on the outskirts of town, plus I had the next day off, and I was looking forward to a hot meal and a warm bed. The music blaring out of the speakers vibrated the cab, the rhythmic beats keeping pace with the adrenaline pumping through my veins. I was more than ready to relax into my weekend.

No sooner had I pulled into my driveway, than my phone lit up, buzzing with an incoming call. It was from a local number that wasn't in my contact list, which normally I might have sent to voicemail, but something told me that I needed to answer this call. I tapped the green phone icon and put the vehicle in park.

"Hello?" I said, pulling the keys out of the ignition.

"Hey," came a nervous masculine voice. "Is this Phil? Phil Mendoza?"

"That's me. Who is this?"

"My name is Andrew Green. You don't know me; I got this number from your sister Angelica."

"Oh ok," I answered, releasing a muted sigh. I already knew were this was going. "How can I help you?"

"So…," Andrew muttered, trailing off for a moment. I knew that tone well; that mix of hesitation and quiet desperation. "I think there might be something strange going on in my house."

Cautiously at first, he began explaining what he'd been experiencing. He was understandably guarded about some of the more unusual details, so I listened patiently, filling any pauses with open ended questions. Eventually he seemed to relax, emboldened from having a sympathetic audience to confide in.

Andrew Green and his wife Denise had lived in a stunning, spacious house on the Northside of Chicago. They'd both spent the better part of a decade turning that property into their absolute dream home; it had been a true labor of love. Andrew was an extremely talented commercial artist and Denise was a high-level executive at a major electronics company. They were both extremely affluent, their success made even more impressive by the fact that they were still relatively young; Andrew and Denise were both in their late 30's.

The couple had a deep love for international travel. Their success had ensured a great deal of flexibility for them both, and they had wholeheartedly embraced this opportunity to see as much as they could of what the world had to offer. Of their many varied destinations, the couple had always been particularly drawn to the countries of East Asia; Thailand was far and away their most beloved destination.

A little over a year ago, just after her 39th birthday, Denise had begun to experience inexplicable health problems. It had started out with various minor symptoms; excessive hair loss, fatigue, and mental fog. They had passed it off as nothing serious, maybe a vitamin deficiency of some kind, and figured it would pass quickly. However, despite an intensified regimen of nutritional supplements and wellness practices, the symptoms not only persisted, but grew worse with each passing day.

Denise, an extremely active woman, who never let a day pass without going to the gym or riding her bike, suddenly found it difficult to muster the energy to get out of bed in the morning. She had become increasingly forgetful and her appetite had drastically diminished. Money was certainly no object for the couple, and her doctor had performed every test conceivable to try and identify the source of what they could only describe as a 'complete loss of vitality'.

A year later, just after her 40th birthday, Denise Green had passed away with Alzheimer's and dementia. In those last few days, she had been so debilitated, that she couldn't even write her own name. A whole team of doctors, who had been recruited over the course of the year to study the medical anomaly, could not ascertain why such an active, physically fit woman in the prime of her life could have deteriorated so quickly. Andrew had been blindsided.

In the days following her funeral service, Andrew had been understandably distraught. The love of his life was gone, and he had no idea what had caused it. He'd also begun to have strange, dark nightmares, which at the time he had attributed to his grief, and thus, he'd reasoned that they would go away in time; but as the weeks trudged on, they had only gotten worse.

He had begun experiencing sleep paralysis and night terrors, which, in the course of his 40 years, he had never been subjected to. Strange, darting shadows had begun to appear throughout the house, and his period of mourning had begun to develop into acute depression. As one who'd never had a history of mental illness, nor a tendency towards superstitions or paranoia, Andrew had begun to suspect that something more otherworldly might be going on.

Initially, Andrew had been hesitant to attribute the events of the last year and a half to anything supernatural in origin; the very notion had sounded like something out of a cheesy horror novel. He'd vowed to keep the stranger details of the phenomena to himself, for fear of sounding delusional. However, when his depression had begun bordering on suicidal, he had decided it was time to reach out for help.

"Do you think you can help me?" Andrew said softly, after a brief moment of silence.

"Yeah," I replied warmly. "I'll see what I can do."

—

Due to scheduling conflicts, the soonest I could make it out to begin the investigation was the following weekend. Because his point of contact had been my sister Angelica, who he'd met on the Chicago art scene, I decided to bring her along. She was also a practiced occultist and a gifted medium. I had complete faith in her ability to handle whatever we might encounter during our visit.

Piles of dead leaves crunched beneath my tires, as Angelica and I pulled into the circular driveway that led up to Andrew's house. The truck was loaded up with everything we might conceivably need to conduct the investigation. For a moment though, I hesitated, taking in the details of the property. Could this really be the correct address?

"Are you sure this is the right place?" I inquired, shooting my sister a sideways glance.

"Yep, this is it," Angelica smirked.

The structure before us was less a house, and more a mansion. It was sprawling and palatial, its massive double doors flanked by ten-foot Corinthian pillars and a vaulted arch overhead. Monumental ash trees towered over the driveway on both sides, their skeleton branches waving at us in the cool October winds. I was rendered utterly speechless.

Once we'd gathered our tools, we made our way to the front door, where Andrew was waiting for us, donning black fitted denim jeans, a light grey V-neck sweater, and a weary smile. His eyes were sunken and dark, making him appear as though he hadn't slept in years.

"Hey, you must be Phil," he said, extending his hand in greeting. "Nice to meet you."

I shook his hand firmly and nodded. "Nice to meet you as well, though I wish it were under better circumstances." Andrew responded with a weak grin and a nod.

"Come on in," he said, gesturing for us to follow him.

The extravagance of the home from the outside, could not have prepared me for the sheer opulence of what awaited me inside. It was plainly evident that not an inch of that home was factory made; this was a painfully detailed, customized haven. The entry way was floored, wall to wall, with high end venetian marble. The walls throughout the home were wrapped in meticulously oiled leather, and the ceilings were gilded in a polished, shining brass. Antique treasures and authentic Asian artwork adorned each room. Every detail had clearly been planned, and I could sense that a lot of love, work, and time and been poured into creating such a unique, beautiful space.

After drinking in our surroundings, Angelica and I followed Andrew into a large, open sitting area, where we set our bags down. While our host went to retrieve some refreshments, we proceeded to unpack our bags and set up the recording devices for our initial interview. Determined to properly document this investigation, I had spent hours the day before, testing my equipment and ensuring that everything had fresh batteries or was fully charged. Digging through my duffel bag, I pulled out two digital cameras, a brand-new digital voice recorder, and my trusty old mini cassette recorder.

Both digital cameras were then mounted onto tripods, each facing Andrew's seat from a different angle. I placed the digital voice recorder on the coffee table nearest to where he would be, and figured I'd hold the analog one myself. Next, I proceeded to test the digital cameras, to make sure they were getting the correct shot, and were ready to go upon Andrew's return. However, when I pressed the power button on the first camera, nothing happened.

I pressed it once more, thinking perhaps I hadn't held it down long enough; still, nothing. Having tested all the equipment the day before, I knew it couldn't be some kind of internal malfunction. Shaking my head in frustration, I walked over to the other camera and hit the power button; still, nothing happened. I would soon find that this was the case for all the recording equipment I'd brought.

By the time that Andrew returned carrying a serving tray, I was still fiddling with my equipment, struggling in vain to figure out what possible reason there could be why all these perfectly functioning devices were suddenly rendered inert. This went on for longer than I care to admit, and finally I just decided to let it go; I'd have to take notes the old-fashioned way, I realized with annoyance.

I fished a tattered old notebook and a ballpoint pen out from the bottom of my bag, and took the seat nearest to Andrew. Jotting down the date and time, and a few quick preliminary observations, I nodded for Andrew to proceed with his story.

A bit reserved at first, Andrew described the events of the last year and a half with as many details as he could recount. Much of it I'd already heard from our initial phone call, but there were a few elements that he'd left out before, such as the sinister content of his worsening nightmares and the peculiar smells and disturbances he'd been experiencing more recently. More than once we had to pause for him to regain his composure. The poor man was clearly still in mourning, and the unexplained phenomena was only adding to his sorrow.

Once we felt we'd gotten as much information as we possibly could from Andrew, we decided it was time to tour the home and see if we could spot anything strange or out of place. Above all, we knew we needed to identify the source of this oppression.

The rest of the house, as expected, was similarly adorned, and just as opulent. The master suite was perhaps the most lavish room in the home, which we passed through to reach the rooms on the far side of the building. It was furnished with an array of exquisite antique dressers and armoires, and an imposing four-post bed. Visually, it was by far the most spellbinding bedroom I'd ever seen, but there was a peculiar sense of foreboding in the air. As I took in the details of the room, one object caught my eye in particular: a miniature replica of a mediaeval castle, seated on one of the dressers closest to the bed, complete with four circular towers, each topped by sky blue domes.

I wasn't quite sure why I felt so drawn to it. Of all the wonders I'd seen in this veritable mansion, it was perhaps one of the least impressive items. It also seemed a bit out of place in a home that had clearly been dedicated to collecting art pieces exclusively from East Asia.

"Shall we?" Andrew asked, calling my attention back to the matter at hand.

"Let's," I agreed, returning my focus to the investigation.

Upon completing our walkthrough, we found nothing specific that could account for Denise's death or any of the other phenomena that Andrew had been experiencing since. Angelica and I exchanged knowing glances, both of us beginning to suspect that this was a man going through an unimaginably difficult time, and that perhaps there was nothing paranormal going on here at all.

As we followed him back through the master suite, I was beginning to regret making the trip, and I was dreading the moment that I would have to tell him that there was nothing that we could do for him; I couldn't remove something that had never been there to begin with. That was when I observed something that gave me pause.

The space on the dresser where the tiny mediaeval castle had been mere minutes ago, was now occupied with what looked like a miniature replica of a Thai pagoda, replete with a sloping roof, golden spires, and it was covered in ornate designs. It appeared to be authentic, an extremely impressive antique, but what had happened to the castle? Was someone playing a game with us?

"Hey Andrew, what happened to the castle that was over here?" I inquired.

"What are you talking about?" he answered, visibly confused. "What castle?"

"The little European castle that was sitting here on the dresser when we came through here earlier." I pointed to the miniature pagoda. "This wasn't here last time."

Determined to get to the bottom of it, I described the details of the castle to him, as thoroughly as I could remember them. Still looking completely bewildered, Andrew finally shook his head and shrugged.

"I honestly have no idea what you're talking about," he muttered, scratching his head. "I've never owned anything like that."

"Who else is in this house with us?" I persisted. If this was some kind of prank, I wasn't getting duped. I was starting to get annoyed, and felt my blood pounding in response.

"It's just us, I live here alone," he insisted, likely sensing my agitation.

At that point, I stopped myself, and took a deep breath. Getting upset wasn't going to help me figure this out. Like a flash of lightning, an inspired idea popped into my head.

"Hey sis," I called out, looking over at Angelica. "Did you bring your pendulum with you?"

A look of recognition lit up her face, and it was clear that she knew why I was asking.

"I did," she chimed, digging the instrument out of her pocket.

She made her way over to the pagoda reverently, as though acknowledging the implication behind my question. With a steady hand, she held the pendulum over the pagoda, and slowly lowered it until it was about a foot from the tip of the roof. Immediately, the pendulum reacted.

At first, the crystal-tipped pendulum began to vibrate wildly. Then, it began to spin in circles, wider and wider until it was spinning on a nearly-horizontal axis around the roof of the little pagoda. Without a doubt, we'd found the source of the disturbance, and right then I suspected I knew what the object's true purpose really was.

"Where did this come from?" I questioned, turning to Andrew with my notebook in hand. A little confused, but willing to cooperate, he told us the story.

A little over a year ago, Andrew had begun his search for the perfect gift for Denise's 39th birthday. His search had eventually led him to a high-end antiques dealer, deep in the heart of the city. His search had ended there, when he discovered the ideal present: a 200-year-old pagoda miniature from Thailand. The saleswoman hadn't gone into any details about its history or origins, but he didn't care; he knew Denise was going to love it.

Of course, as Andrew had suspected, Denise was enamored with the gift. It was precisely the kind of present that one gets for someone who can buy herself anything she could possibly want; it was priceless. Her birthday festivities had come and gone, and afterwards, the couple busied themselves planning their next visit to Thailand, inspired by Andrew's stellar gift. Unfortunately, that trip was never to take place; within the span of a week Denise's health had begun to decline, resulting in her tragic death a year later.

By now, I was in a stunned silence, and I could feel a lump forming in my throat. How was I going to break the news to Andrew that this sincere gesture of love had been the key to the death of his beloved wife? I knew what that little box was, and the person who sold it to Andrew must have either not known or not believed in it, because it wasn't really a gift at all.

What Andrew had purchased in that antiques dealership was not just a novelty replica of a Thai pagoda, but was actually something called a spirit box, or spirit house. Many of the Thai people place them in strategic areas outside of the home as an homage to the resident spirits of the area. They leave libations and offerings for those patron spirits, in order to appease them and recruit their help in warding off the more malevolent ones. It was essentially a haven for non-corporeal entities, and as such was never meant to be brought inside the home. On top of that, it had probably not been 'fed' in quite a while; certainly not during its stay in the Green household.

Unknowingly, Andrew had brought a ravenous, disembodied spirit into the home, and had given it to his wife. Unappeased, this spirit was quite literally feeding off of Denise's life force, bent on survival and on maintaining its foothold in the physical world.

Poor Denise, I thought. *But also, poor Andrew.* I looked over at Andrew, who looked absolutely miserable, and lost as to why we were so focused on such an innocuous, yet sentimental object.

"Look Andrew," I sighed, carefully formulating my diagnosis. "I'm perfectly aware that you gave this to your wife with the best of intentions, but this isn't just a curio object; this is a spirit box, with a very specific function." Taking a deep breath, I explained to him what the nature of this miniature pagoda really was.

"If you truly want these disturbances to stop, you'll have to get rid of this thing," I emphasized, wrapping up my detailed explanation.

At first Andrew appeared horrified, but that soon evolved into a reluctant sadness. He was quiet for a moment, and then shook his head in denial.

"You don't understand," he protested. "This was the last present I ever gave her. It's hers. I can't even conceive of parting with it."

I cringed inwardly. "Ok, I get it," I responded in resignation. "But I promise you, until you get rid of this thing, the torment will not stop."

Recognizing that we'd clearly come to an impasse, we wrapped up our investigation, packed up our things, and headed home.

———

I returned to his home quite a few times after that, checking in on him, and trying to gently persuade him to destroy the object; all to no avail. Unfortunately, I'd been correct about the disturbances; not only did they continue, but they increased in their aggression and frequency. Yet still, the more I tried to convince him to part with it, the more he dug in his heels, and there was little I could do.

Eventually, one snowy December morning, I received a phone call from Andrew: he was finally ready to dispose of the pagoda. When I asked him what had convinced him, his answer chilled me to the core.

His nightmares had taken a dark new turn. Now, they consisted of graphically vivid depictions of him peeling the flesh off of his own body, over and over, until only a bloody, dripping skeleton remained. Apparently, that was all the motivation he needed.

That very same day, according to the directions I'd given him, he removed the object from the house, took it apart, piece by piece, and burned it. He reported an immediate sense of relief afterwards, and in my communications with him since, I've been informed that all phenomena have now ceased. For the time being, my job at the Green household was done, and I could rest easy knowing that I'd succeeded in helping someone.

When an entity has hooked itself onto a specific person or item, it quickly goes into survival mode, especially if it senses a threat. More often than not, it operates using a form of low-level mesmerism, or hypnosis. It endears itself to those who encounter it, creating a parasitic spiritual bond. As a result, its host is extremely reluctant to get rid of it.

Andrew's sentimental devotion to the Thai pagoda was in many ways completely understandable, which made it much more difficult to convince him to part with it. It symbolized his deep devotion to Denise, and the adoration that she'd felt for the object amplified its continued importance in Andrew's life. Unfortunately, this perfectly reasonable attachment was the ammunition the entity used to ensure its continued presence within the Greens' home.

In the beginning, I suspect Andrew was also in denial about the object being the culprit behind Denise's death and the later strange activity in their home. That is also a function of an entity operating subtly on the human subconscious; it's much easier to remain in control, if the host doesn't recognize the object as the source of the oppression to begin with. Soon after, I saw the spirit's hand in Andrew's refusal to get rid of the pagoda. The item had become highly precious to him, and for quite a while, he acted as its guardian. Based on the obvious wealth the Green's had at their disposal, the monetary value of the item was irrelevant, and I can't imagine that the price tag had any bearing on Andrew's decision. These types of phenomena tend to create a cognitive dissonance within their host; even though a person may genuinely believe that an object is the culprit behind the negative activity the person is experiencing, they are attached to it at an emotional level, and become desperate to hang onto the item.

Another more general example of an entity at play, as with Jessica's case prior, is the egregious amount of scheduling conflicts that arise. Somehow, it becomes impossible to find the time to go through the process of ousting the negative energy. Things come up unexpectedly, and oftentimes the person being affected by the oppression becomes notably resistant to actually carving out time in which to take care of the situation. These are all just a few of the patterns that, at the time, I was just beginning to take notice of.

Nevertheless, I counted this case as a success; I'd done all I could, and I was glad that now Andrew could process his grief without the meddling of lower energies. My reverie was short-lived, however, because from that moment on, the calls for help began pouring in.

Case Study 3: Dave

The sky was awash in the glowing embers of the setting sun, the electric hues of pink and violent hanging heavy on the horizon, as I sauntered over to my truck. Preparations for the Vernal Equinox ritual were finally complete, and I'd gone out to stretch my legs and to check my phone. Reception was notoriously spotty inside the building, and I needed a brief reprieve before the ceremony officially commenced. My fellow Temple officers had carpooled to a nearby fast-food restaurant for burgers before the rest of the Order members arrived, and I'd opted to stay behind to let them inside and get them mentally prepared for the ritual.

I was silently contemplating the lines from our upcoming ritual, and dwelling on the currents of rebirth and rejuvenation that Springtime offers. A light breeze rustled through the trees, and though the air was still cool, there was an undercurrent of warmth, carrying with it the promise of summertime and new growth. Leaning against my truck, I scrolled through notifications on my phone, taking intermittent sips from my water bottle.

An incoming call engulfed the screen, forcing me to pause my scrolling. It was from a phone number that was not in my contacts, but due to the impending festivities, I answered it anyways. I had been designated as a point of contact for any new Order members who might have questions prior to tonight's ritual, and I'd agreed to make myself available to them. With a quick swipe, I picked up the call.

"Hi, is this Phil Mendoza?" the caller inquired.

"Yes, it is, how can I help you?" I chimed warmly.

"My name is Sandy Wilson," replied the female voice, in a subtle, midwestern accent. "I got your number from the owner of Gypsy Haven; they told me you were the person to talk to about getting rid of ghosts and things like that."

Gypsy Haven was a local occult bookstore that I frequented. I'd also been doing geomancy readings there on the weekends, and had developed a great relationship with the owner. They'd referred many clients to me over the years, which at times could be both flattering and overwhelming.

"That's one way to put it," I chuckled lightheartedly, conjuring the mental image of myself in a Ghostbusters jumpsuit, a proton pack strapped to my back, vacuuming up wayward spirits. "How can I help?"

Sandy had barely begun to respond, when a line of cars began pulling into the parking lot, many of which I recognized as attendees for the evening's event. I apologized for the interruption, and Sandy was as gracious as can be expected, but I could tell that something was worrying her. I promised to return her call first thing in the morning, and resumed my duties as Temple officer for the evening.

—

The following morning was shrouded in a blanket of cloud cover, the threat of an impending thunderstorm seemingly imminent, as I plopped down on the sofa with my notebook to return Sandy's phone call. This time, it wasn't Sandy who answered, but a distinctly male voice.

"Hi," I started hesitantly. "I'm returning a call from a Sandy Wilson; is she available?"

"She is, may I ask who's calling?"

"My name is Phil, Phil Mendoza."

"Oh!" came the enthusiastic response. "I know who you are! She told me she was gonna call you. I'm Dave, Sandy's husband."

What followed was roughly two hours of Dave bouncing from story to story, detailing the plethora of supernatural phenomena that had been occurring in their home. In fact, he was so excited about the odd activity, that I wasn't entirely sure why they'd reached out to me; Dave didn't seem bothered by it at all. However, I could frequently hear Sandy in the background, correcting Dave's recollection of the events, and it became increasingly evident that it was Sandy who wanted the activity to stop; not her husband.

Dave and Sandy were a warm, friendly couple, in their early 40's, with no children, and one small dog, which would occasionally bark in the background. Sandy was a substitute teacher, and Dave worked in a production warehouse. Both of them were extremely social, and they hosted game nights on a regular basis; they were also both die-hard Cubs fans. Dave had the erratic, excitable demeanor of a Jack Russell Terrier, and Sandy was clearly the one who ran the show.

Over the last few months, strange phenomena had begun manifesting all around the house. Initially, the activity was limited to random flashes of bright lights, much like the flash on a camera, but with no perceivable cause. Before long, glowing orbs of various colors started showing up as well. Most recently, they'd caught sight of shadowy figures moving around the rooms. Additionally, as if he needed to prove himself, Dave proudly informed me that he had caught quite a bit of the activity on film.

Ever since they'd first started experiencing the phenomena, Dave had begun amassing an impressive collection of video footage, chronicling as much of the activity as possible. He had none of the usual trepidation of my typical clients; he wasn't at all concerned with my reception of his claims. While I was glad that he didn't appear to be upset or afraid of what was going on, a deeper concern began to blossom in the back of my mind. Dave acted like a kid in a candy store when discussing these events, and I knew how easily admiration of the spirit world could turn into an unhealthy obsession.

So far, none of the activity seemed especially menacing, but I was also well aware that many times, this is how the phenomena escalates; these entities play on a person's ego and create a connection that seems meaningful to them, in order to latch onto a host. Of course, I couldn't be certain of any of it just yet, but I took note of it all the same.

Dave and Sandy lived in a local rowhouse, sharing walls on both sides with their neighbors, and once Dave described it, I knew exactly where they lived. It was less than a five-minute drive from where I was, so I decided to go ahead and do a quick investigation that same day.

As I pulled up to the house, the morning's storm clouds had begun to roll back, allowing beams of sunlight to pierce through. The shining sun filled me with optimism, and I began the short walk up to their front door, where Sandy stood waiting for me.

She was a heavy-set woman, with sandy blonde hair and commanding blue eyes. Sandy was a thoughtful woman, with a decidedly serious demeanor; she spoke with the directness and confidence of someone who naturally takes charge of any given situation. At her request, I removed my sneakers in the foyer, and followed her into the living room.

Before we reached Dave, I could already hear the infectious laughter echoing down the hall. Turning a corner into the living room, I was greeted by the image of a man who could have been the real-life inspiration for Ned Flanders from The Simpsons; that is, with a much more receded hairline. He had a slender stature, stood at about an inch shorter than his wife, and now appeared to be vibrating with wonder.

"Check this out!" he cried, gesturing for us to join him.

As I followed his gaze, I was shocked to see a spherical orb, roughly the size of a golf ball, glowing a fluorescent green, floating a few feet in front of him. I blinked hard, and looked around the room, trying to find the source of the anomaly, but could find nothing to explain it. It took me a moment to process what I was seeing, and before I could say a word, Dave reached out towards the ball of light.

"Don't touch it!" Sandy snapped.

"Just watch," Dave replied dismissively. By now, the object was but a few inches away from him, and he began waving his hand back and forth, in a semi-circle motion. Then, for a few surreal minutes, the glowing sphere drifted left to right and back again, seeming to mirror Dave's movements; it appeared to be interacting with him, quite deliberately.

I was admittedly dumbfounded, in that moment. What exactly was my role here? This wasn't the typical kind of investigation that I was used to. Though I was still fairly new to this type of work, most of the calls I'd gotten thus far were full of desperation; they were terrified, and rightly so. In contrast, Dave seemed to be thoroughly enjoying the phenomena. An exasperated sigh from Sandy pulled me from my train of thought.

"Why don't we go ahead and do a quick walkthrough, and then we'll all sit down and talk about what's going on," I suggested diplomatically. Sandy nodded and gestured me to follow, seemingly grateful to leave the room.

As we made our way through the first floor, nothing of any particular significance stood out to me. I had no doubt that something supernatural was occurring in their home, but I had yet to pinpoint its origin; there were none of the usual tell-tale signs. However, the second floor was a different story.

Each step that I took up the stairs took more and more effort. The air around me felt heavy, and it got worse the higher we climbed. By the time we reached the top, the gravity of the energy felt like an iron curtain, and I was feeling winded and impossibly heavy. I took a moment to stabilize myself, peering down the hallway.

We walked the short distance to the master bedroom at the end of the hall, passing the bathroom on our left, the only other room on the second floor. The master bedroom itself was of modest size, well-kept and fairly typical; a few dressers, a king-sized bed on a metal frame, and a set of double doors marking the closet. The only unusual aspect of the entire tour was the fact that I was still having trouble with the density of the energy; it felt as though I had weights attached to my ankles. Exiting the master bedroom, on our way back downstairs, I caught sight of a rosary hanging from the doorknob, strung together with dark blue marble beads.

"Are you Catholic?" I asked, pointing at the rosary.

"Sort of," Sandy shrugged. "We used to attend Mass pretty regularly, but not so much lately."

I nodded in response, following her back down the stairs. The orb was gone by the time we returned to the living room, and Dave was gazing pensively out the large bay window at ash grey clouds that had begun forming in the distance.

"Find anything?" he asked, shooting us an uninterested, sideways glance.

"Nothing specific, no," I replied. "Why don't we sit down for a few minutes?"

Taking my suggestion, they both took their seats on the sofa, though Dave seemed a bit reluctant. Overall, they seemed like a healthy, well-adjusted couple, but I could already feel the activity in the house driving a wedge of silence between them.

"Obviously there is something supernatural going on here, you don't need *me* to tell you that," I offered finally, breaking the tension. "What exactly would you like to see happen here? What do you need from me?"

"I want it to stop," Sandy replied flatly, glancing at her husband, who was carefully avoiding eye contact. "It scares me."

"Dave?" I prompted, looking directly at him.

"I don't know," he muttered, shifting uncomfortably in his seat. "It's not really hurting anything, and it's really entertaining. But at the same time, I don't want Sandy to be scared or worried."

Timidly, he reached out and took his wife's hand. It was a disarmingly tender moment between them, and her gaze softened as she looked at him. She leaned over and kissed him gently on the cheek before returning her focus to me.

"When can you start?"

———

Over the course of the next few weeks, I made several visits to Dave and Sandy's home. I performed my sets of banishing and prayers each time, which seemed to settle much of the activity, but a few days later it would return. Through divinations and my own experiences in the house, the stronghold of the phenomena was definitely on the second floor, but I still wasn't entirely sure what the phenomena actually was or where it had originated from.

It went on like this for a while, until I stopped hearing from them, and I assumed that the activity had ceased. I hadn't heard from them in two solid months, and their case had drifted to the back of my mind, as I became busy with other cases and the daily tasks of my own life. Then, late one evening, I received Sandy's distressed phone call.

I had just planted myself on the couch with my family, eating pizza in my pajama pants, when I heard the chime of my phone from the kitchen where I'd set it to charge.

"Dad, someone named 'Sandy' is calling you," my daughter informed me, returning to the couch with a plate of food. Curious to see what could have prompted her to reach out after months of silence, I made my way to the kitchen and picked up the phone.

"Hey Sandy, what's up?" I answered cheerfully.

"I don't know what happened," she began frantically. "Dave is acting extremely out of character, and that rosary we had hanging on the bedroom doorknob has been spinning around and around for the last hour, and this is really freaking me out. Please, I need you to come help me."

I groaned internally and swallowed the bite of pepperoni and cheese I'd just taken. Deliberating carefully, I decided I couldn't abandon her at that point; the fear in her voice was troubling, and she didn't strike me as someone who was easily spooked.

"Ok, give me a bit to gather my things, and I'll be there," I replied finally, attempting to mask my hesitation with an equal level of sincerity.

An hour later, I pulled up in front of their house. From the street, it looked like every light in the house was on, and the energy already felt dense and somehow frenetic, as if Dave and Sandy were hosting a massive party. Perplexed by this feeling, I walked up to their front door and rang the bell.

Almost immediately, Sandy answered the door, her eyes heavy with stress, and her hair frizzy and disheveled. She looked like she hadn't slept in years.

"Come on in," she mumbled, moving to the side.

"Oh hey Phil!" came a manic shout from behind Sandy. Dave waved me cheerfully inside, his thinning hair standing on end in some places, and an animalistic look in his eyes.

The entire house seemed to buzz with movement, and the air was thick with static electricity. In the living room, the television was on, though muted, playing a foreign black and white movie silently in the background. All the furniture seemed slightly askew, as if it had been moved around and haphazardly put back in place. However, the oddest detail of all was Dave himself.

He was wearing a green short-sleeved, button up shirt, but the buttons weren't lined up correctly, and his jeans, though clean, looked severely wrinkled, as if they'd been left in a ball on the floor for a few days. At first, he paced back and forth at the base of the stairs. Then, he seemed to forget what he was doing, and walked in and out of the kitchen several times, muttering to himself. Suddenly, his eyes lit up as if he'd just remembered something.

"Phil, you have to see this," he insisted, in a strained, high-pitched voice. "I got something the other day, and I thought of you, come on!"

Dave made his way to the stairs, almost skipping in his enthusiasm. Looking back at me, he gestured for me to follow him; he was trying to get me to go upstairs. I felt an impending sense of dread, heavy in my chest.

"Why don't you bring it down here, Dave?" I offered strategically. "I just got here, and I was hoping to sit down and visit for a few."

A look of indignation passed over Dave's face, almost imperceptibly.

"I can't, you have to come up here to see it," he insisted. "It's really cool, you're gonna love this."

"I'd really rather not man, just sit down so we can talk" I responded, holding my ground. I knew all too well that whatever was happening in this house, the base of operations was on the second floor; it would have the upper hand if I went upstairs, and I could not allow that to happen.

"Come ooooon," Dave continued to beg. "I promise, you won't regret it!"

At that moment, I felt myself beginning to get angry. I'd left the comfort of my own home, and abandoned the precious little time I got to spend with my family, to help this couple. I was in no mood to play games.

"Look Dave," I snapped. "You're gonna listen to what I'm telling you or I'm gonna get the hell out of here and you can figure this out for yourselves."

"CUT THE SHIT, DAVE," Sandy roared, clearly reaching her limit with her husband. "I'm sick of this, sit down and let Phil do his job!"

Obediently, Dave made his way to the sofa, head hanging like a dog that had just been reprimanded. Once he'd finally composed himself, I began my banishing ritual.

I decided to begin my work in the kitchen, as it was on the far side of the house, near the back door. Initially, everything seemed to be going smoothly. As I completed my work in each area of the home, I could feel the entity's grip weakening, and I had started to feel confident that my work would be completed very soon. I decided to return to the living room to see how Dave and Sandy were faring, and my new found confidence disappeared.

"He's been doing this ever since you started," Sandy said with tears in her eyes, as she rubbed Dave's back comfortingly.

Dave was shaking violently, and mumbling something under his breath that sounded like complete gibberish to me. His eyes were open, but looked glazed over and vacant. I waved my hand in front of his face, but he didn't seem to register what was going on at all.

"I'll go ahead and start the banishing in here now, maybe that will help," I said tentatively, fighting against the distinct feeling that something was about to happen. No sooner had I began my litany, than Dave sprang from the couch and tackled me, screaming in a fit of rage.

Sandy, who was following right behind to try and stop him, collapsed on top of me as well. Soon, the three of us were rolling around on the floor, fighting for control. Sandy and I struggled to pin Dave down and stop him from seriously injuring both of us. For such a slight man, he was shockingly strong, though I doubted that level of force was coming from him.

I smacked my head on a side table, trying to avoid getting a fist to the face, and all the furniture around us went flying. The sounds of our scuffle were sure to draw attention from the neighbors if we didn't get this under control quickly. The last thing I needed was to have the police show up; there'd be little chance of finishing my banishing then.

For a brief moment, I was able to spin Dave around so that he was lying face down, and I pinned his arms behind his back. Face first in the carpet, he began growling something that I couldn't make out, so I loosened my hold slightly and let him lift his head. What I heard next defied logical explanation, and made my blood run cold.

Dave opened his mouth, and his eyes rolled all the way back, so that his pupils were no longer visible. What followed was a sound that I knew was not physically possible. He appeared to be speaking, but I couldn't make out any of the words, because multiple voices escaped his throat at once, speaking in a variety of pitches and tones. It was like listening to numerous frenzied conversations all at once, but they were all coming from one man. Nothing I'd ever learned or experienced could have prepared me for this horror, and for a moment that felt like an eternity, I was in complete shock.

Taking advantage of my stunned state, Dave threw his head back, attempting to knock me off the back of him. I slid back just in time, keeping one knee in the small of his back, and looked behind me to check on Sandy, who was fighting to keep his legs pinned down.

"Don't let his feet go, he kicks like a mule!" she cried. "He has a black belt in Aikido!"

Just then, I noticed something I hadn't before; a whole series of framed photographs lining the mantle above the fireplace. In each photo, Dave was in a series of martial arts poses, including shots of him midair, one leg extended, about to strike his opponent.

You've gotta be shittin' me, I thought grimly. *This just keeps getting better and better.*

Finally comprehending the gravity of what Sandy was telling me, I repositioned myself and helped her restrain his legs, which had already begun jerking violently, trying to thwart our grasp. It took every ounce of strength that I could muster to keep him down. Both Sandy and I were literally sitting on his back, which should have been more than enough to subdue this slender man, yet somehow, he very nearly threw us both off more than once.

For a brief moment, Dave's struggling subsided, and he twisted his head to the side to look back at me.

"Do you know why you're here?" he asked, in a low, sinister voice that was not his own.

"You know what, why don't you just tell me," I retorted. I was at a loss at this point, and was quickly getting fed up with this violent dance.

"Because we knew you'd come," the voice returned, dripping with malice. "And now, you're FUCKED."

Fan-fucking-tastic, I thought bitterly. *It said 'We'; there's more than one spirit at play here.*

As if responding to my thoughts, they spoke again, working Dave like a puppet. Multiple voices chattered simultaneously, in some sort of insidious, discordant harmony, before synchronizing once more.

"Do you wanna see how strong WE are?" they crooned in a wicked purr.

In a flash, Dave flipped over, wrenching one hand free of my grasp. Luckily, Sandy had adjusted quickly, and returned to sitting on his legs. I immediately braced myself for the inevitable impact of Dave's well-honed punch, but to my surprise, he reached out for the nearby coffee table.

One of the finer pieces of furniture in Dave and Sandy's home was a five-foot long, rectangular coffee table, made of real mahogany. It was clearly not a factory-made, particle board piece; this had been made by hand. It was a solid, heavy piece of furniture, well over 100 pounds, that would have taken at least two people to maneuver well; that is, unless you've been overtaken by a host of non-corporeal entities, desperate to assert themselves on the material world.

Wrapping one hand firmly around the leg of the table, Dave effortlessly lifted it into the air such that each leg was perfectly level, and over a foot off the ground. I sat for only a second, gaping at the grotesque display of power. All the color had drained from Sandy's face, when I turned back to check on her. The situation was escalating quickly, and I was reaching the limits of my knowledge on how to counteract it.

A harrowing cackle escaped Dave's throat, that was at once both primal and eerily childlike. These beings were enjoying my struggle, feeding off of my reactions. In that moment, I felt completely lost, and they embraced the opportunity to take advantage of it. In one fluid motion, Dave dropped the table and grabbed my shirt, pulling me down to face him. Without warning, he leaned forward, mouth agape, and attempted to bite me.

The struggle to keep Dave pinned down recommenced, and I had to straddle his stomach, using the entirety of my body weight to keep his top half on the floor. I ran through every prayer I had memorized, called on every Divine Name I could possibly think off, while he gnashed his teeth angrily at me, spitting and cursing at me in unfamiliar voices.

A quick glance down at my watch told me that I'd been engaged in this physical conflict for over two hours, and there was still no end in sight. Realizing that I was quickly running out of options, I pulled the bottle of Holy Water out of my pocket, popped the cap off, and proceeded to pour it down Dave's throat, holding his jaw in place with my free hand.

Hoping the sanctified contents would trickle into his system, and loosen the entity's hold on Dave, I continued on in this manner for a while. Not wanting to empty the entire bottle just yet, I set it aside, ignoring the preternatural growls that were now emanating from the poor man underneath me. The hold was loosened, but he wasn't free just yet.

Exhausted and running out of options, I slapped Dave across the face; still no response other than the same irreverent laughter from before. I splashed him once more with Holy Water, and struck him again. I repeated this process several more times, until finally he cried out in surprise, in his own voice.

"What the hell are you doing Phil?!" he gasped, his eyes clear once again, scanning the room in confusion. "Get off of me!"

"I've had just about enough of you, you son of a bitch, you just sit still for a minute," I commanded. "Sandy, is it him?"

"It is! It is!" she exclaimed triumphantly. Confident that Dave was free of the invading spirits, I stepped off of him and collapsed onto the floor, while Sandy embraced her husband once more, tears streaming down her cheeks. Every muscle in my body ached, and sweat was pouring from my forehead. Suddenly, I remembered the rosary upstairs, which Sandy had reported spinning in circles earlier, so I sprinted up the steps to check on it.

Upon inspection, I found it dangling lifelessly from their bedroom doorknob, and I made the mistake of reaching out to grab it. Immediately I dropped it on the floor, and saw the welts forming on my palm; the rosary was burning hot. Grabbing a washcloth from the bathroom to wrap it in, I picked it up, and took it back downstairs with me.

Though I wasn't entirely sure what the nature of that rosary's involvement was in the phenomena, I suspected that the entity had been hiding inside of it, so I decided that it was for the best if I disposed of it properly. Pouring the remaining Holy Water into a bowl, I dropped the rosary into it and let it sit for a few minutes. Then, I snapped it in half, and put the broken pieces, now cool, into a Ziplock bag to take with me.

Much to my and Sandy's surprise, Dave couldn't remember a single moment of our Thunderdome-style wrestling event. All that he could recall was hearing his wife answer the door, and then regaining awareness pinned beneath me. Where had his consciousness gone during that time period? I had a multitude of questions, but for the time being, they would have to remain unanswered.

While Dave recuperated on the sofa, tended to by one elated Sandy, I completed the banishing throughout the rest of the house successfully. Once he had regained his composure, I gave him some follow up advice, to help him avoid this course of events in the future. We chatted for a bit about spiritual hygiene and the importance of balance and finding his spiritual path and truly embodying it.

"If I were you, I'd be in church every day of my life after this," I advised him with all the intensity I could muster. He seemed to accept this, and shook my hand gratefully.

"Absolutely," he responded gratefully. "This won't happen again."

—

The next morning, I felt like I'd been hit by a freight train. My skin was riddled with scratches and bruises, and a gnarly bump had begun to form under my scalp. I was grateful that I'd been able to help, and that no one had been seriously injured, but I vowed to be much more careful next time, and considered how I might better prepare for cases like this one in the future. I was also learning quickly that there were definite limits to the type of help that I could provide.

A few weeks later, Dave contacted me, reporting that the phenomena had resumed. It was incredibly disheartening to hear. However, when I asked him if he'd followed any of the instructions that I'd given him the last time we were together, he dismissively responded that he hadn't. Regrettably, I informed him that I could no longer work this case. I had done my part in their home, but Dave had refused to do his, and I couldn't put myself in danger a second time for someone who wasn't going to do the necessary work. It was one of the most difficult conversations I've ever had in this line of work.

This case was unique in a variety of ways. Although I couldn't count it as a success per se, as I hadn't been able to fully evict the oppressing entities from the Wilson home, it was a learning experience, and highlighted many important points that need to be addressed. The first lesson I've taken from this case is the proclivity of spirits to prey upon the human ego.

We live in an increasingly mundane world, where events that defy physics and logic are few and far between. When Dave began witnessing these phenomena, he was mesmerized, entranced even. The more that he successfully interacted with them, he felt special, almost magical; he acted as if he'd been chosen for that 'gift'. The rapport he'd developed with them solidified their hold, making him increasingly resistant to ridding himself of their influence. This danger, of entities appealing to the human ego, thoroughly informs another important cautionary point.

It is no big secret that I have been doing ceremonial magick for a major portion of this earthly life. While much of that work focuses on developing and evolving oneself, it also involves working with spiritual beings outside of oneself. Thus, I am not claiming that spirit work is always a negative, dangerous activity; it can be very rewarding and a vital source of personal and spiritual growth. However, like with any hobby, one must find balance.

The difference between obsession with the spirit world, and working with that realm in the scope of one's magickal practice, is both subtle and nuanced. In any ritual setting, where one is working with non-corporeal entities, clear boundaries must always be set. You are inviting them in to converse and learn from them; not to move in indefinitely. You are the sovereign being in your own life, and if you begin to lose control over your words and/or actions, it is time to withdraw and reevaluate the work you are doing, and what it is you truly want to get out of it. Otherwise, like Dave, you may find yourself a hapless victim, and a tool for beings who likely don't have your best interests at heart. Similarly, the importance of good spiritual hygiene cannot be emphasized enough.

There is no single path to truth or enlightenment; there are many. What matters is finding the belief system that resonates with you, and truly embodying it. Dave and Sandy were originally Catholic, which is why one of my pieces of advice to him, after that final struggle, was to return to his faith. This is not because I believe Catholicism is the one true religion, but because it is a valid system of spirituality, that works for many people. If someone is inclined towards Buddhism or Wicca, for example, I would encourage them to embrace that fully.

As humans, we long for something more, something beyond ourselves, and it leaves a kind of metaphysical void in our spirit. If that void is not filled with something that makes us feel a soul connection to something much grander than we are, something will always come along to fill that void. Whether it is substance abuse or an obsession with the spirit board, we always find a way to achieve that connection. The question is really a matter of whether or not that connection helps us to lead more fulfilling, enriching lives.

The final lesson in all of this is not relegated to the spiritual world, but to all things. As a person, I am naturally predisposed to helping others; it is something that I choose to do whenever I can. In this case, I learned the hard lesson that you cannot help those who will not help themselves. You also can't help those who do not want the help you are offering. Dave didn't truly want to be rid of the spirits, and thus, he didn't adhere to the instructions that I left him with. That was his decision to make, and I would never hold that against him. However, I had put myself at risk for serious injury working his case, and I could not do that again if he was not willing to do his part.

That was one of the very few cases in which I have had to decline further assistance. It is rare, but it does happen, and it is always a difficult decision for me to make. Fortunately, once I learned how important it was to set my boundaries when working cases such as this, I was better able to manage the toll that some of these situations take on me, both mentally and spiritually, and have become a far more capable practitioner because of it.

Phil Mendoza & Patricia K. Reyes

Case Study 4: Lisa

T he shadows cast by the fire shivered and danced, creating an enchanting backdrop for the gentle glow of the twinkling lights adorning our tree. Christmas carols drifted softly from the speakers, engulfing my living room in a festive ambience. It was Christmas Eve, and my family was gathering on the sofa, preparing to open one present each; a recent tradition we had come to honor.

"Hurry up, Mom," my son groaned from his corner of the couch, a brightly wrapped package clutched tightly in his arms.

"Almost ready," my wife replied with a smile, as she wiped cookie crumbs off the kitchen counter.

"You know," I interjected playfully, pouring a glass of merlot. "If you'd have cleaned up after yourself, we'd be opening presents already."

"Your father has a point," added my wife, amidst heavy sighs from both children. With a smirk, my wife took her glass of wine from the counter and made her way to the living room.

Switching off the lights in the kitchen, I grabbed my glass and went to join her, when I heard my phone vibrating on the sideboard. Assuming the only calls I'd be getting on Christmas Eve would be from friends or family, I swiped to answer without reading the Caller ID.

"Merry Christmas," I answered cheerfully, fully immersed in the spirit of the holiday.

"M-Merry Christmas," a female voice answered, seemingly confused by my familiar greeting. "Is this Phil? From Gypsy Haven?"

Shit, I thought, biting my lip. *Should have let it go to voicemail.*

"It is," I responded, mentally switching gears. I glanced over at my wife, who was already eyeing me suspiciously. "How can I help you?"

"My name is Lisa," she began. "I am so, so sorry to be calling you on Christmas Eve! I would have waited, but something really terrifying just happened, and I don't know what else to do."

"It's ok," I assured her. "Tell me what's going on."

Lisa was the manager of a strip club on the edge of town, and her husband was a long-haul truck driver, who was on the road at the time. They had two sons; one was 4 years old, and the other was 17. For as long as she could remember, Lisa had been prone to periods of bad luck and random clusters of bizarre accidents. It had been her running joke that she was 'cursed', or that she had two left feet, and hadn't thought much of it. Unfortunately, much to Lisa's dismay, this particular string of bad luck was turning out to be far worse than it had ever been before.

The scent of rotting food and burning hair constantly engulfed their home, though she could find no explanation for it. Additionally, the temperature had been fluctuating wildly from room to room, regardless of the season. One night, her youngest son had complained that his bed was moving on its own while he was trying to sleep, which initially she'd attributed to an overactive imagination. All of these events she'd taken in stride, and while the severity of the phenomena was certainly unprecedented, it didn't feel especially dangerous; that is, until that fateful Christmas Eve.

Earlier that day, Lisa had been relaxing in her living room, bundled up in her easy chair, as she was recovering from a surgical procedure on her shoulder. She'd had the house to herself, and had flipped through channels on the television before settling on an old black and white Christmas movie. She'd reclined the chair and shut her eyes, hoping to doze off for a bit, when a muscle in her leg had sharply cramped up.

Letting out a yelp of surprise, she'd tried taking some deep, relaxing breaths, attempting to ease what felt like severe muscle cramps in her leg. Glancing at the television, which was still playing the opening scenes of It's a Wonderful Life, she'd shrugged it off, and tried once more to get some sleep. However, before she could even close her eyes, what felt like a large human hand clamped down on her calf, gripping it tightly.

Immediately, she'd jerked forward to see who or what had grabbed her, and found that she was still alone in the room. When she'd looked down at her leg, to try and figure out where the sensation was coming from, her breath caught in her throat: there was a reddened imprint on her flesh, in the shape of a massive hand, which wrapped all the way around her leg. She'd screamed in alarm, and attempted to jump out of the chair, but was instantly pinned back into her seat. The phantom hand around her leg then released its hold, only to wrap itself around her neck, choking her in an iron grip.

That was the last thing she remembered before she'd blacked out. Upon regaining consciousness, she'd checked the time, and her heart dropped; she'd been knocked out for 3-1/2 hours! She'd been filled with a sense of dread at the idea that something invisible could so easily overpower her. She had children, and she couldn't allow this to escalate any further. That was when she'd decided to make the call.

An uncomfortable silence lingered in the air. Helping people with these kinds of problems was something that I was deeply committed to, but it was also Christmas Eve, and my family had just settled in to enjoy our time together.

"Please…" Lisa begged. "My sister is dropping my son off any minute now, and I'm worried that he'll be in danger. I don't know what else to do."

I thought carefully for a moment, shifting my weight from one foot to another, and looked over at my family. My son and daughter were chattering excitedly with one another, arguing playfully about who had the most presents. My wife was finishing her glass of wine and scrolling through her phone absentmindedly. At face value, her actions seemed innocuous, but I could feel her patience with this conversation thinning.

I didn't want to go. I wanted nothing more than to stay home and enjoy Christmas with my loved ones. At the same time, I'd made an unwavering commitment to this work. I tried putting myself in Lisa's shoes; certainly, she would also like to have a warm, safe holiday season with her children. With an internal sigh, I downed my glass of wine, desperately wishing that it was something stronger.

"Ok," I finally caved. "Text me the address and I'll be there in a bit."

—

Tufts of snow had begun to fall, which crunched beneath my tires, as I pulled into Lisa's driveway. It had been nearly two hours since her phone call, as I'd had a heated discussion with my wife before leaving the house. Understandably, she hadn't been pleased that I was taking a job on Christmas Eve, and I'd had to smooth it over with both her and the kids, promising another bottle of wine and a pint of ice cream upon my return.

Lisa lived in a fairly new gated community on the other side of town. It was a two-story home, with a spacious, well-lit front porch, despite the fresh snow piling up around it. The temperature outside was dropping rapidly, and I pulled my jacket tight around me as I walked briskly up to her front door and rang the doorbell.

44

"Hey Phil," she said with a weak smile, swinging open the door and gesturing me inside.

Lisa was a tall, slender woman in her mid-30's, with dark hair and piercing brown eyes. She carried herself with the sharp confidence of someone who has navigated more than a few tragedies in her life, and has decidedly persisted.

As I pulled off my thick winter boots, so as not to track melting snow into the house, I took in my surroundings. The interior was elegant, tidy, and tastefully decorated. A short, artificial Christmas Tree sat glowing in the corner of the living room, and a digital Yule Log blazed across the huge flatscreen TV mounted on the wall.

"You have a beautiful home," I remarked with a warm smile.

"Thank you," she replied, the corners of her mouth twitching slightly. "Where do you want to start?"

"Let's do a quick tour of the house, then we'll sit down and discuss," I suggested.

The investigation of the home itself was largely inconclusive. Lisa's youngest son was now home and sleeping soundly, and her oldest was up late, playing video games on his computer, so we decided that there was no need to disturb either of them for the time being. While the kitchen and other areas of the house that we explored were as lovely as the living room, nothing in particular stood out to me as having any paranormal significance. In fact, the only space that stood out was the closet in her bedroom, which was the final stop on our tour.

The master suite, located on the second floor, was massive, and furnished in dark mahogany and dark shades of burgundy and forest green. As expected, everything was immaculately organized; it was clear that Lisa took a great deal of pride in her home. The only things that stood out to me were the double doors that led to her closet, and although I hadn't inspected any of the other closets in the house, I felt the need to take a quick look inside this one.

As soon as I stepped into Lisa's sprawling walk-in closet, it felt as though I'd entered a vortex of static electricity. The hair on my arms stood at attention, and I could feel the infinitesimal shocks as I shuffled across the carpet. I wasn't certain what to make of the strange phenomenon. The energy swirled and pulsed like a cesspool of electrical charge, and I knew instinctively that something unnatural was taking place in there. However, this offered me no definitive answers as to what exactly it was, so I decided to do a quick divination to get to the heart of the matter.

Once we'd returned to the living room, I cast a quick circle of protection, and proceeded to divine the source of the disturbances. After sitting with the results for a few minutes, it was clear that whatever was going on here was rooted in something that had happened a very long time ago.

"What happened in 1997?" I asked. Lisa, who was waiting quietly in her easy chair, shifted uncomfortably, and crossed her arms over her chest.

"Nothing I can think of," she shrugged, glancing away.

"Nope, that's not gonna work," I countered firmly. "I'm not trying to get in your business or be nosey or anything like that. I'm just trying to help you and figure out what's happening here, but if you're not interested, it's Christmas, and I have places to be." Once more, she insisted that nothing of significance had taken place that year. At this point, I was beginning to get frustrated.

Beyond a shadow of a doubt, I knew that my divinations were accurate, and her defensive body language had further confirmed it. It also occurred to me that whatever had happened might have been subconsciously repressed, so I decided to put her under a light hypnosis, and try to access the information that way.

Using the Calendar Regression method, I slowly took her back in time; first, to the previous week, next to the previous month, and proceeded further and further back. After a few minutes of this, we eventually regressed her memories all the way back to the events of 1997.

Not long after her 16th birthday, Lisa had begun dating a boy from her high school. He would soon become her first sexual partner, as the relationship quickly became intimate. A few short weeks later, she'd discovered that she was pregnant. Although Lisa had been raised Catholic, she was well aware that she couldn't handle having a baby at such a young age, and had decided to terminate the pregnancy.

Months had passed uneventfully, and her life as a high school student proceeded normally, until one day she'd been dumbstruck by a frighteningly vivid illusion. In it, she'd been shown her unborn baby, tormented and broken, in graphic detail. Its tiny body looked as if it had been chopped into little pieces, and it cried out to her through a mangled, bloody mouth, begging for its mother.

Immediately, Lisa had fallen into an emotional tailspin. It had been 1 year to the day since her abortion, and the guilt that she'd carried with her had finally reached a tipping point. The vision had felt like a knife in her heart, and to her, it had proved her absolute culpability in the affair. So, convinced that she was doomed to carry that pain for the rest of her days, she then decided to take her own life.

While both parents were still asleep, she'd snuck into their bedroom. Swiping both her father's car keys and a full bottle of nitroglycerin that he took for a heart condition, Lisa had slipped out of the house and driven to the nearby market. There, she'd purchased a single red rose, and proceeded to swallow the entire bottle of her father's pills. In her last remaining moments of consciousness, she'd floored the gas pedal and crashed into a ditch just off the highway. That was where she'd eventually been found, holding the rose up towards the sky, as if asking for forgiveness from God. By the time emergency services had found her, she'd gone into massive organ failure, and had to be rushed to the hospital.

They were eventually able to stabilize her, but she'd fallen into a vegetative state, and the doctors had to inform her family that there was nothing more they could do. After a brief deliberation, Lisa's parents had then made the difficult decision to take her off of life support, and a priest was quickly brought in to give Lisa her Last Rites. Much to everyone's surprise, as soon as the priest had completed his litany, Lisa began to stir and her vital signs began improving. The attending physician had been completely baffled by this odd turn of events; for all intents and purposes, she should not have been able to survive the overdose. Her case had been dubbed a 'medical miracle', and Lisa made a full recovery.

From that point on, although she had pulled through, a string of inexplicable bad luck and freak accidents had followed her, culminating in the paranormal phenomena that she'd recently begun experiencing. Somehow, breaking the taboos inherent in her Catholic faith, first the abortion, and then her suicide attempt, had created a gateway for something otherworldly to latch onto her and exert its influence over her, well into adulthood. Finally, we had gotten to the root of the oppression that Lisa, and to a lesser extent her family, had been subjected to. Now, it was time to get rid of that disembodied parasite.

Once I brought her out of that hypnotic state, I quickly divined the entity's name. Using the methods of Solomonic magick, I summoned it into my circle of protection, and banished it from Lisa's life permanently. The process went as smoothly as could be expected, and by the time I finished, she reported that she felt lighter, and a peace fell over her that she hadn't felt in a very long time. My work there was complete, and I returned home to spend the rest of the holiday with my family.

—

In the weeks that followed, I heard from Lisa occasionally, and I am proud to report that there have been no further disturbances. Desiring a fresh start, her and her family soon made the decision to move; not only to a new home, but to a whole new state. Confident in my divination abilities, Lisa asked me to do a reading for her, concerning what state they should move to.

They'd narrowed down their options to either Arizona or Florida, so I decided that the best method would be to use my pendulum. Pulling out a map of the United States, I started by suspending the pendulum over Arizona. The answer came back as a huge negative; this destination was clearly not the ideal place for them to settle down. Next, I held the pendulum over Florida.

It quickly became evident that Florida was the most desirable option of the two. My pendulum kept centering over a city south of Orlando, called Kissimmee, and over the St Cloud area just southeast of it. Lisa was shocked by this, as it turned out that she'd actually lived in Kissimmee for a few years back in her 20's. However, her heart was clearly set on Arizona.

Weeks later, Lisa flew out to Arizona to scope out the area and look at some houses. Within the first 48 hours of her visit, she was bitten by a Brown Recluse spider, and wound up hospitalized for an entire week. Undeterred by the experience, Lisa and her family ended up moving to Arizona. I heard from her one last time, after they had moved and settled into their new surroundings. According to her, everyone was doing just fine, and I was very happy to hear that.

Divinations are guideposts for our lives, and we are always free to follow our own path, and subsequently to navigate the consequences of those decisions. Lisa made the choice that she felt was best for her and her family, and I am glad that I had a hand in releasing the burden of her past, so that she could move on and begin this new chapter in her life.

Phil Mendoza & Patricia K. Reyes

Case Study 5: Hazeem

The piercing rays of the afternoon sun blazed down onto the asphalt as I hopped out of the truck, assaulting my face with a merciless wall of summer heat. Even for July, the air was thick and oppressive, as I entered the second half of my shift. My crew was replacing a stretch of underground pipe systems for a nearby oil refinery, and though I'd been a pipefitter for years, sweltering days like that one still had me pondering my life choices. Retrieving my cooler from the trunk, I made my way to the worksite.

As I maneuvered safely around an excavator that was busy unearthing a buried pipeline, I almost missed the delicate chime of my cellphone, alerting me of an incoming call. It was from a local area code, and I decided to answer it on the way to my assigned station.

"Hello," came an articulate, female voice. "My name is Mahaila; may I please speak with Philip Mendoza?"

"This is he," I responded, plugging my left ear against the sounds of grinding gears and the incessant hum of industrial labor.

"I was referred to you by one of your former clients," the woman began, with a very faint, unidentifiable accent. "She told me that you were very good at getting rid of evil spirits, is this true?"

"It is," I confirmed, silently amused at my blossoming reputation around town.

"I believe there may be something sinister taking place in our home," she began. "Would you be able to help me with this?"

"Absolutely," I assured her. "I'm actually at my day job right now though. Can I call you back this evening and we can go from there?"

"Yes!" she exclaimed gratefully. "I will make myself available. And thank you."

—

Later that evening, once I was finally able to catch up with her, Mahaila relayed to me what had been going on in her home. Her and her husband, Hazeem, had only been married for a couple of years. While they were very much in love, their marriage had been turbulent from the start, due to a longtime heroin addiction, which Hazeem had suffered from ever since emigrating to the United States as a teenager. Though at times he'd been able to manage his addiction, he could never quite seem to fully recover from it.

Due to her husband's illness, Mahaila was admittedly grateful that they had not had any children yet. Hazeem had a passionate interest in high-end men's fashion, and he had invested most of his time and savings into pursuing a career in that arena. While he was clearly destined to become a master of his craft, attempting to maintain any kind of consistent progress, while navigating the highs and lows of his addiction, had proved nearly impossible. That, coupled with the prejudices surrounding Hazeem's Pakistani heritage, had made his pursuits extremely difficult.

While I sympathized with their situation, regarding Hazeem's battle with addiction, I wasn't entirely sure what my role was here. My services are spiritual in nature; I am not a drug addiction counselor, nor am I a licensed therapist. That was when she informed me of the strange phenomena that had been occurring within their home.

Initially, the couple had been awoken at all hours of the night by strange sounds in the home. Having no children or pets on which to blame the disturbances, they'd thought it peculiar, but had left it at that. However, as the weeks flew by, the unexplained sounds had become increasingly repetitive. The sounds eventually morphed into a repeated ticking noise, much like the sound produced from winding up a toy or a music box; just an inexplicable, rhythmic clicking.

Neither of them had suspected that something supernatural was at work, based on this phenomenon alone, though they had yet to find its source. They had both pushed the experience to the periphery of their minds, as it hadn't felt particularly menacing either. Eventually, they'd written the noises off; that is, until one day, something terrifying took place, which deeply disturbed them both.

One evening, while eating dinner, Hazeem had stopped talking mid-sentence, and a shadow passed over his face. After a few seconds of silence, Mahaila had attempted to regain his attention, but to no avail. Hazeem, who at that point had slumped over in his seat, appeared to have passed out. Quickly, Mahaila had flown to his side. With a few gentle pats on the cheek, she'd attempted to revive him, but as she turned his head to face her, what she saw made her blood run cold.

Hazeem's facial features had somehow morphed into a form that was altogether different. His eyes, though closed, had become dramatically sunken. The contours of his nose and cheekbones had shifted from their usually rounded curves, into sharp, angular lines. Even his jet-black facial hair had paled to an ash gray color. Before his wife had been able to process that bizarre development, Hazeem's eyes flew open, and Mahaila's voice caught in her throat.

Although the tawny brown of his eyes hadn't changed like the rest of his face, deep in the center of his pupils blazed what appeared to be two tiny flames. Shocked by the whole affair, Mahaila had instinctively jumped back and away from her transformed husband, lost her balance, and struck the back of her head on the corner of the kitchen cabinet.

Seemingly reacting to his wife's cry of pain, Hazeem had lurched forward, shaking his head, as if to clear it, and his features returned to normal. He'd leapt from his seat to tend to his wife, and helped her up, stroking her face lovingly. He seemed to have returned to normal, and he remembered nothing of the last few minutes. It had become second nature, ignoring the weird noises around the house, but the events of that nightmarish evening had been far too harrowing to simply brush aside.

"I am not sure if there is something evil going on in my home," Mahaila concluded finally, in a weighted tone. "But I would like to know for sure, so that we can take care of it. I do not want this to get any worse."

"I agree," I responded reassuringly. "Let's find a time when I can come out, and I'll see what I can do."

—

A few weeks passed before I could make the trip out to meet Mahaila and her husband. They were living in Chicago at the time, and summertime is an exceptionally busy season in my line of work. I'd had to put it off until my crew had wrapped up our current project, and I'd finally managed to squeeze in the short trip late one Friday afternoon.

Their home was situated in an affluent neighborhood on the northside of the city. The walkway up to their front door passed through a veritable garden of potted plants, replete with all manner of flowers and meandering vines. The alluring scent of jasmine and hyacinths engulfed my senses as I rang the doorbell. It was Hazeem who answered.

Hazeem was a man of average height, with a carefully groomed beard and a piercing gaze that belied his jovial nature. His charcoal slacks were perfectly ironed, as was his pinstriped, obsidian dress shirt, which showcased an expertly starched collar, and a pair of understated, titanium cufflinks. It became immediately clear to me, based on Hazeem's meticulous sense of fashion, that he had chosen the right profession. He greeted me with a broad smile and a firm handshake, before inviting me inside.

In the foyer, a short row of shoes was lined up against the wall, just to the right of the doorway. To the left, was an ornate screen, with geometric shapes carved lovingly into what appeared to be authentic mahogany, partitioning off the entryway from the living room. The living room itself was clean and simple, furnished with low rows of seating cushions, and an equally low coffee table.

The entirety of the home was similarly decorated. Minimalist accents adorned each room, which were covered in soft fabrics, with occasional geometric patterns and pointed arches. Splashes of green highlighted an otherwise neutral color palette, and the only exception to this was the sprawling Turkish rug in the dining room, incorporating deep reds and golds into an otherwise uniform color scheme.

Once we'd exchanged pleasantries, and taken a quick tour of the home, Mahaila joined us in the living room and took a seat. She wore a modest, navy-blue pantsuit, and a forest green hijab, with gold embroidery around the edges. Though she spoke very little during my visit, she carried herself with a quiet confidence, and did not hesitate to assert herself when necessary.

Both Hazeem and Mahaila were extraordinarily hospitable and easy to talk to. More than once, our conversation led away from the purpose of my visit, and the topics ranged from religious beliefs to sports. I felt extremely welcome in their home, and found no evidence of anything out of the ordinary taking place. In fact, at one point, Hazeem pulled out his copy of the Quran, from a delicately carved wooden box, and read a few verses from it. Lovingly, he turned the pages, his hands encased in white silk gloves. Although I did not know what the Arabic verses meant, his rich baritone vibrated and lingered reverently in the air.

We eventually reached a slight lull in the conversation, and I decided to take that moment to discuss the reason for my visit. I hadn't really found any evidence of spirit activity in the home thus far, and I wasn't sure that my services were needed here. However, the look of concern that crossed over Mahaila's face made me feel uneasy, so I decided to do my typical divination, before coming to any definite conclusion. The first bit of information I received was a name, which I'd never heard before.

"Who is Faizan?" I inquired.

All the color drained from Hazeem's face, and he eyed me suspiciously for a moment. I knew I'd struck a nerve with that name, so I waited patiently for him to formulate his answer.

"How do you know that name?" Hazeem finally responded.

"Whoever that is, they had something to do with what's happening to you right now," I explained. "And, to get to the bottom of this, I need to know who Faizan is."

After a brief, uncomfortable pause, Hazeem explained to me that Faizan was one of his uncles. He'd lived next door to Hazeem and his family back in Pakistan, and was around for most of his childhood. According to Hazeem, Faizan had been both a gifted sorcerer, skilled in Islamic magick, and a violently abusive man.

Neither women nor children had been immune to his brutal assaults, including his own wife and daughters; and, more than once, Hazeem had been on the receiving end of his uncle's rage. He didn't offer many details on this, but judging by the change in his demeanor, it was clear that the memory of his uncle's cruelty had been forever burned into Hazeem's mind.

As if Faizan's physical abuses hadn't been enough, he'd also made Hazeem an unwilling participant in certain magickal workings. Between the divination, and my own intuition, it was becoming clear that both Faizan's magick, and the extreme trauma that Hazeem had sustained from his abuse, had opened a gateway for whatever was taking place. However, there was still one more piece of information I needed from him.

My divination pointed to an event that had taken place when Hazeem was around 11- or 12-years-old. While Faizan had opened the door for whatever was going on, something else had happened to Hazeem at that age, which he was still feeling the effects of. When I asked him about it, the spark of recognition that lit up his face told me that he now knew exactly what was going on.

When Hazeem had been a young boy, still living in Pakistan, there was a small lake near his village, which he'd loved to frequent. One day, while standing by this particular body of water, he had been overcome by an invisible entity, which he called a 'jinni[1]'. Scared out of his mind, he immediately ran home to his parents for help.

In the days that followed the incident, his mother and father had begun to observe strange behavior in their son. Periodically, he would start speaking in multiple different languages, none of which he could have possibly known at the time. He would make startlingly accurate predictions, about events that he would have had no way of knowing. However, the account that really got my attention, was that when these episodes had taken place, his physical appearance would change.

These phenomena didn't last long, before his parents had contacted the local shah about their son's condition. The shah, along with an imam and some other religious clerics, had arrived a few short hours later, and proceeded to exorcise the jinni from young Hazeem. After a day or two of prayer, and other Islamic exorcism techniques, the crew had departed, declaring that the jinni had been successfully expelled.

---

[1] The jinn are a class of non-corporeal creatures, existing within the Middle Eastern belief systems. These beings preceded Islam, though they were later incorporated into its mythology, as their existence was considered a matter of fact, not fiction, among the Arabic peoples.

A year or so later, just after his 13th birthday, Hazeem had emigrated to the United States with his family. Although, the previous symptoms hadn't resurfaced until very recently, he'd suffered from a crippling heroin addiction ever since. In and out of prison for drugs and other drug-related crimes, he'd tried desperately to establish himself in this country, but he was beginning to feel like it was a losing battle. He hadn't associated his addiction with the possession he'd experienced as a boy, because he'd genuinely believed that the jinni had been exorcised; until now.

Confident that the jinni had not been completed ousted from my new friend, with his permission, I decided to attempt some basic banishing prayers that same afternoon, in an attempt to see what it was I was really dealing with. Although I no longer identified as Christian, most of the entities I'd dealt with previously seemed to be rooted in Christian paradigms, and in my experience, they all seemed to answer to the same authority; specifically, the name of Jesus Christ. However, I was not prepared for the response I was about to receive.

Beginning my litany, I spoke a quick prayer, and commanded the jinni to leave Hazeem, in the name of Jesus Christ. As if triggered by my spiritual probing, a change passed over Hazeem's face, and his features slowly morphed right in front of my eyes. It was clear that I was no longer speaking to Hazeem the person.

"I have existed far longer than that prophet," growled the jinni, speaking through Hazeem. "He has no command over me."

I was floored. I'd known that this case, if it indeed proved to have a supernatural component, might be more difficult to navigate than previous cases, due to my lack of knowledge regarding Islamic beliefs and traditions. Additionally, I had very little knowledge of the jinn, and had certainly never encountered them before in my magickal practice. Perhaps for the first time in doing this work, I was completely out of my element.

I performed a quick banishing in their living room, which seemed to offer Hazeem some temporary relief. He soon regained consciousness and his features returned to normal. Still, I knew that to permanently remove the possessing spirit, I was going to have to do some pretty extensive homework. After promising to contact them once I had a plan of action, I took my leave and returned home.

—

Over the course of the following weeks, I immersed myself in learning about the Quran, Islamic practices, and how the jinn fit into that pantheon. There was a definite precedent within the teachings of Islam regarding the possession and expulsion of the jinn, and a whole plethora of varying beliefs on why they attack humans and what their place is in the hierarchy of creation.

I was wholly unfamiliar with the Arabic language, so there were definite limits to the work that I could do within the Islamic system itself. As an outsider to the Islamic faith, I had to get creative in dealing with the jinni oppressing Hazeem. Ultimately, it was the Hindu goddess of death and rebirth, Kali, who was actually able to get the job done.

Once I'd divined the individual jinni's name, I evoked the being into manifestation, using the occult methods I'd been trained in. The entity appeared before me, as clear as day, wrapped in gray rags, and wearing a fiery red headdress. Its eyes were empty spaces; two dark, ephemeral voids. Finally, I invoked the dark goddess Kali, and charged her with ousting the stubborn jinni.

I stood my ground in that space for hours, as I witnessed the dark goddess perform her magick. The air hummed with electricity, and before my eyes, sparks of light snapped all around the shadowy entity, searing it away piece by piece. Each pinpoint of light picked away more and more of Hazeem's oppressor, until finally the jinni dissolved into a faint pillar of smoke and disappeared.

Since then, Hazeem and Mahaila have experienced no further phenomena in their home. Hazeem is now in recovery, and they are expecting their first child very soon. Both his marriage and his career are now flourishing.

I had no idea, when embarking on this journey, that I would be coming face to face with a jinni, in a suburban neighborhood of the American Midwest. While this undertaking wasn't nearly as dangerous or intense as some of the others, it was certainly one of the most unique. It was my first cross-cultural case, and a profound reminder that supernatural phenomena are not isolated to any particular culture, belief system, or religious creed.

Case Study 6: Gloria & Nathan

The deep thump of the bass vibrated the walls, as sound and light reverberated off of the vaulted ceiling. Through the skylight above, the moon peered down at me, glowing and full. It was the day after Christmas, and I'd been invited to attend a party hosted by Erin Black, a good friend of mine, who also happened to be the head of the Massage Therapy Department at the local community college. So far, I'd seen a few familiar faces at the event, but aside from my host, I didn't really know anybody.

I took sips of chianti from my glass, as I meandered through the crowds, mingling and introducing myself. Most of the guests in attendance seemed to know one another, which came as no surprise; all of them were either classmates or faculty. However, much to my surprise, some of them seemed to know me.

"Hey, do you know a woman named Gloria?" asked a young man, who'd introduced himself as Jacob, with thick glasses and wide eyes. "Gloria Jensen, she's one of our classmates."

"I don't believe so…" I responded, taken a bit off guard. "The name is vaguely familiar, but I can't be sure."

"Hmm, well, you need to meet her," Jacob added knowingly, before wandering off to find the girl he'd arrived with.

Apparently, this woman Gloria was on everyone's mind that night, because I was asked six more times about her, by people I'd just met. Everyone seemed to know about the spiritual services I performed, and for whatever reason felt like Gloria was someone that I needed to meet. It was unanimously decided that we would all discuss her once the party died down, and most of the guests had gone home.

Over the span of the next few hours, the crowd slowly thinned out. Heavy with red wine and hors d'oeuvres, I planted myself in an overstuffed armchair while Erin escorted the last of the guests to the door. All that remained were a select few students and faculty who knew Gloria's story, and who seemed dying to tell me about it.

"Ok, I think that's everybody," Erin declared, returning to her sprawling, tastefully decorated living room. "Thanks for sticking behind Phil. I thought it best, for the sake of Gloria's privacy, that we keep this between those of us who already know her situation."

"It's no problem," I assured her, with the wave of my hand. "What's the deal with Gloria?"

"Gloria is one of my students," Erin began with a sigh, plopping down onto the sofa opposite me. "For the last few weeks, she's been missing a lot of classes, which isn't like her at all. She's set to graduate next semester, so I pulled her aside to see what was going on, and ask her if she needed any extra help with her coursework. That's when she shared what was happening with her son, Nathan."

"Poor kid's only six years old," added Serena, a middle-aged woman with short hair, who I'd known for all of 3 hours.

"He's certainly at the age of active imagination," Erin nodded. "But this feels like more than that. For weeks now, he's been too terrified to sleep in his own bed at night. He tells his mother that there are monsters coming to get him, that they're pulling him out of his bed at night and trying to take him away. So, he's been sleeping in his parents' bed almost every night, and Gloria has been getting very little sleep because of it."

"I asked her if he could have watched a scary movie or something that might have triggered it, but she couldn't think of anything," Jacob interjected.

"It's wearing on her," continued Erin. "She's normally an excellent student. Between that and the weird electrical issues with her house, she almost didn't pass her classes this semester."

"Electrical issues?" I inquired; my curiosity was officially piqued.

"Yeah, they keep having power surges, and random outages," Erin explained. "And for some reason, it's just *their* house. No one else in the neighborhood has been having trouble."

"I see, that *is* very weird," I mused. "But why are you telling *me* about this?"

"She's beginning to think that something... otherworldly is going on," responded Erin, choosing her words carefully. "I don't know what to believe; all I know is they need help, and you're the only person I know of who is equipped to get to the bottom of it."

"Ok," I replied, finally understanding the urgency. "Let me know how to get a hold of her, and I'll see what I can do."

—

After a brief game of phone tag, I was able to catch up with Gloria the following weekend. Immediately I could tell that she was an exceptionally sincere person, and a devoted mother. Her concern for the welfare of her son eclipsed her trepidation at sharing some of the more bizarre aspects of what had been going on. I began our discussion with the alleged electrical disturbances; as someone who works in construction, I thought it best to rule out any basic wiring problems in the house.

According to Gloria, her husband had called out a whole team of electricians and engineers to survey their home and find the source of the issue, and none of them could find a single reason why the problem was occurring. And, just as Erin had reported, not a single other household in their neighborhood had experienced any problems with their power in the last few years. It was becoming more than just a nuisance; it was starting to become costly.

The erratic power surges had fried more than one of their electronics. Their home desktop computer had simply stopped working, and just a few days before I got in touch with her, Gloria's laptop had started smoking and had to be replaced. She'd lost a good portion of her assignments when that happened, so not only was she losing money, she was also losing time, as she had to redo a handful of essays that were due the following week. The electrical issues alone were enough to completely disrupt her family's life; however, power fluctuations were the least of her concerns, as I would soon discover.

In general, Gloria's husband, Jeff, and her 10-year-old daughter Sara, hadn't experienced any strange phenomena; aside, of course, from the electrical issues. Gloria herself, who had spent more time in the home than either Jeff or Sara, claimed that the house frequently felt oppressive and heavy. Personal items would seemingly disappear, only to be found later in a completely different room. Nevertheless, it was easy to write these things off as forgetfulness or stress on her part. More concerning than these more subtle occurrences, was the fact that Gloria and her husband had been at each other's throats for the last couple of weeks.

According to Gloria, her and Jeff had always been a laid-back, easy-going couple, who'd rarely had so much as a disagreement. However, for reasons neither of them could think of, they had been concluding most of their evenings with shouting matches. Jeff had even raised a fist to her earlier that week, in a fit of anger, and she was quickly becoming concerned, not only for the safety of their marriage, but her own physical safety as well. As if all of these things weren't enough to make her feel like she was losing her mind, she was also deeply concerned for her youngest child. The one who seemed to be feeling the full weight of the phenomena was her young son Nathan, who I would soon learn was at the source of the oppression.

As I'd learned at Erin's party the week before, Gloria confirmed that Nathan had been having horrible nightmares about 'monsters' who were trying to abduct him, and had taken to sleeping in his parents' bed most nights. What Erin hadn't told me, likely because she hadn't been aware of it, was that Nathan had indeed been pulled out of his bed at night; at least twice that Gloria had been aware of. In fact, that was what had prompted her and Jeff to allow Nathan to start sleeping with them.

Late one night, right around 3am, Jeff and Gloria had awoken to the sound of Nathan's blood-curdling screams coming from his bedroom. They'd burst through his door, to find him thrashing on the floor a few feet away from his bed, tangled up in his bedsheets. The room had been ice cold, which they soon discovered was because all three of his bedroom windows had been thrown wide open.

The Jensen family lived in an older home, which still had its original windows. The thick glass in those older models made them extremely heavy and very difficult to open. Little Nathan was just a waif of a boy, barely tall enough to reach the latches on his windows, much less have the strength to open them all the way. Stranger still, was the fact that his bedroom was located on the second floor, so the possibility of a human intruder was all but ruled out. The most perplexing factor of all, was that the screen had gone missing from one of his windows; the same window that he'd happened to be closest too when they found him that fateful night.

At first blush, this hadn't seemed particularly telling; it was just a window screen. Still, the more her and Jeff had surveyed the scene they found their son in, the weirder it all became. The screen was made of a heavy-duty mesh, and was constructed such that it could only be removed from the inside. So, they had surmised, maybe Nathan removed it in a fit, or while sleepwalking; but if that had been the case, where had it gone?

They'd scoured Nathan's room, pulling out all the dresser drawers, and turning over his mattress, looking for where he'd hidden it; they found nothing. Jeff had then thrown on a jacket, grumbling about having an early start the next morning, and patrolled the perimeter of the house with a flashlight, certain he'd find it in the bushes below Nathan's window. An hour later he'd returned, empty handed.

In fact, over the days that followed, Jeff had combed through every bit of the surrounding landscape, but to no avail. He and Gloria had continued to search inside the house as well, and still there was no sign of it. The screen, which had been securely in place just a few days prior, had completely disappeared, without a trace.

For some reason, this detail stuck with me. It seemed innocuous enough, but something about it kept tugging at me. Physical objects don't just dematerialize; at least, not without some form of paranormal influence.

After that night, the unexplained phenomena had seemed to subside. After a few days of peace, Gloria had pushed those memories to the back of her mind, and proceeded with her life as normal; that was, up until one, seemingly ordinary Wednesday morning.

Nathan had finally slept through the night in his own bed, and Gloria silently hoped that perhaps the strangeness was finally coming to an end. Feeling hopeful, she'd made Nathan's breakfast, and went upstairs to get him up. As is common with children of that age, he'd been especially fussy that morning, and kept fighting her as she tried to dress him. At last, exasperated, she'd sat down next to him on the bed, taken his hand, and asked him what was wrong.

In a gesture that was extremely uncharacteristic of her normally affectionate son, Nathan had yanked his hand away. Animalistically, he'd recoiled, sliding backwards and away from her. Then, his head snapped around to face her, and he'd let out a low, grating hiss. His eyes had gone completely black, as if they'd been replaced by two obsidian marbles.

For the first time in her life, and she hoped the last, Gloria had been both fearful *of* her son and fearful *for* him. After that, she could no longer deny that something unnatural was happening to Nathan. Both time and money had become a rare, precious commodity for her family, and she'd had no idea where to start.

A visit to her local parish had proved unhelpful; the only advice they'd given her was to 'pray about it', as if she hadn't already been doing that in earnest. Although her husband was concerned for Nathan, he'd seemed to think it was just a phase, that would pass with time. Jeff also worked long hours as a factory worker, and hadn't had to deal with the issue firsthand, nearly to the extent that Gloria had. She was officially out of options, and feeling more isolated with each passing day.

At this point in our conversation, I was already convinced that I would need to go investigate the home. Unless she was lying about all of it, which I had no reason to suspect, this case was almost certainly supernatural in nature, and was clearly escalating. I'd already resolved to help her out, and I promised to arrange a time to go and see the house, once I'd had a chance to look at my calendar. But, just before disconnecting the call, Gloria had one more detail to add.

"Oh, before I forget," she remarked. "Nathan drew a picture of these so-called 'monsters' he says are coming to get him. It doesn't make any sense to me, but for some reason I feel like I should show you."

"No problem, text it to me after we hang up," I said. "Anything that might be relevant is always helpful."

Less than a minute after hanging up the phone, the image of Nathan's drawing popped up on my screen. At first, I had to double check who'd sent it, because it was an image that I had become intimately familiar with; it was an image that I'd used extensively in my occult studies and practices, and it was almost inconceivable that a 6-year-old could have created it.

The picture was a sketch of the Kabbalistic Tree of Life, expertly drawn, in crayon. The Tree of Life is an archetypal rendering, meant to represent the different stages of the creation of the universe, according to esoteric Judaism. It is composed of ten spheres, or 'sephiroth', each one connected to the rest via 22 lines, or 'paths'. That image alone would have been shocking, considering it was drawn by a child who would have no way of knowing its structure, much less its significance. Nevertheless, in addition to the traditional Tree, he'd drawn another one, connecting to it at the base, and spreading downwards, as if perfectly mirroring the upright version; the significance of this was not lost on me.

In the teachings of Jewish mysticism, for each of the life-giving sephiroth, was a mirrored 'qliphoth'; a word that literally means 'shell'. These qliphoth are shadows of the sephiroth, intelligences of pure darkness. In more modern occult circles, the qliphoth have come to be equated with what some would refer to as 'demonic' entities; quite literally, they are the hidden, shadow side of creation. In short, Nathan had drawn an esoteric, archetypal image, expressing both the light and dark aspects of our reality.

This alone was outrageous, and as hard as I tried, I couldn't come up with a logical explanation as to why a child had drawn something that even most adults would have no knowledge of. To make the situation even stranger, upon closer inspection, I was startled to find a sun sketched at the very top center above the 'trees', complete with squiggly lines for its rays. It was colored completely in black. This further bewildered me.

The image of the so-called 'black sun' is a very specific one, sometimes associated with darker occult practices. It is also an image that often appears in dreams and visions of people who are going through a deep depression, or a 'dark night of the soul'. At the very least, it isn't a particularly positive image; and, coupled with the inverted Tree of Life, it painted a dismal scene.

The final details of Nathan's artwork were a group of shadowy, amorphous beings, emerging from the inverted, qliphothic Tree. They were colored in a dark, smoky black, with blood-red dots for eyes. According to Gloria, Nathan told her that these harrowing entities were the ones who had been coming for him at night.

I was utterly floored by this surprisingly detailed depiction of Nathan's disturbances. This young boy had very accurately portrayed a very ancient, very specific map of reality, and where his oppressors had come from. Based on this, and the persistent electrical issues the family had been experiencing, I knew that I would need to act fast. Without another thought, I surveyed my calendar, and worked out a date to conduct the investigation.

—

The following Thursday, I gathered up my tools, and loaded them into my truck. It was a crisp afternoon in January, and the barren branches of the trees around my house sagged beneath the weight of freshly fallen snow. Kicking the loose powder off my boots, I stepped into the foyer of my home, waiting inside for my sister arrive.

I was bringing my sister Angelica with me on this case. She was a fellow occultist, and gifted in using her pendulum. Additionally, she was a naturally gifted medium, and her skills at seeing otherwise invisible entities had only been sharpened over time. Based on the intense nature of Nathan's condition, I felt it was best to have another person around to provide insight, and another set of hands to help with any workings I might need to do. As punctual as ever, she pulled up to the curb in her little blue sedan exactly one minute early. Quickly, I locked the door behind me and went to meet her by the truck.

"Hey sis!" I called out. "Thanks for coming with me on this!"

"No problem," Angelica smiled, tossing her jet-black bangs out of her eyes. "Are we ready?"

"We're good to go," I confirmed, giving her a quick hug. "Climb on in!"

The drive to Gloria's home in Barrington should have only taken half an hour, but with the icy roads, slick with snow, it took us closer to 45 minutes to get there. They were situated in an older neighborhood, tucked away at the end of a cul-de-sac. From the outside, the brick house appeared to be well cared for, and the sidewalk had recently been shoveled and salted. The only remaining remnant of the holiday season was the welcome mat, which read 'Welcome to our Ho-Ho-Home', with a winking cartoon Santa Claus painted on it.

Just as we reached the front porch, we were met by Gloria. She appeared to be in her early 40's, with jade green eyes, and fiery auburn hair, twisted into a bun. Her eyes looked tired and her smile was strained, but she was genuinely happy to see us.

"Come on in," she gestured, stepping aside to let us through the door. "Jeff's at work, and Sara is at a friend's house, so it's just us."

"Is Nathan here?" I queried, kicking off my boots.

"He is, but my mom will be here any minute to pick him up," Gloria said, stuffing her hands into the pocket of her oversized hoodie. "If you wanna go wait in the living room, I'll make us a pot of coffee, and we can chat until he leaves."

Angelica and I made our way into the living room and took a seat on a large, faded sofa, placing our tools at our feet. The home was clean, and modestly furnished. A faint pine smell hung in the air, presumably from the scented candle at the center of the coffee table. Preemptively, I pulled a notebook out of my bag, and switched on a small lamp that sat on a side table near the couch. From outside, came the muffled honk of a car at the end of the driveway.

"Nathan!" Gloria called out from the kitchen. "Come on down, Grandma's outside waiting for you!"

Seconds later, the quiet sound of socks on the staircase descended, and a tiny figure with a mop of thick, sandy brown hair came into view. Ever the doting mother, Gloria took his hand and walked him to the front door.

As Nathan trotted through the living room, pulled along by his mother, he peered over at us. Out of instinct, I gave him a wide smile, and waved cheerfully in his direction; what I was met with fully unnerved me.

For a brief moment, our eyes locked. He didn't smile back at me; he simply stared, unblinking, as if seeing right into my soul. His youthful, light brown eyes pierced a hole right through me. His gaze was icy, and full of malice. I felt a shiver run down my spine, and reflexively looked away. In that moment, the lamp I'd switched on flickered, almost imperceptibly, and I almost jumped out of my seat.

Now, I've seen a great many things in my life, and in the work that I do; the kinds of things that would terrify even the bravest of humanity. Nonetheless, the look of pure hatred that emanated from that child may be the most chilling thing I've ever witnessed. I was supremely grateful that he was leaving.

Once Gloria returned to the living room, and the three of us drank our coffee and exchanged pleasantries, Angelica and I commenced our investigation of the home. Our tour of the lower level of the home didn't yield any significant results. I had a distinct feeling of being unwelcome there, but I thought it might have been a residual vibration from the death stare Nathan had given me, only minutes before. However, when we took our survey up to the second floor, where all of the bedrooms were located, that feeling of repulsion intensified.

The air upstairs was freezing, even though I could hear the furnace running. There was a distinct sense of being pushed back, as if I were walking against a current. I couldn't yet put my finger on exactly what was at play here, but I wanted desperately to run out the front door, and get as far away from that house as I could. Something did not want us to be there.

Unsurprisingly, Nathan's bedroom felt like a meat locker. I swore I could see my breath in the frigid air, as I took a few cautious steps into that space. Angelica pulled her cardigan closed, wrapping it around her body, and I rubbed my hands together, as we made our way methodically around the room.

"Sorry about the temperature," Gloria offered weakly. "We keep turning up the heat, but this room just never seems to get warm."

"It's ok," I assured her, nodding knowingly at my sister. "Is this the window you were talking about, the one with the missing screen?"

Gloria nodded in affirmation, as I began visually scanning the casement. There were no scuffs or scratches, to indicate any kind of tampering. The energy that churned around it was repellent, but there were no visual cues as to why this particular window should be the source of so much attention. Given the severity of what was going on in the house, and with poor Nathan, I knew there had to be an energetic doorway here somewhere. Intuitively, Angelica pulled out her pendulum, and dangled it near the window pane.

Initially, the pendulum appeared to bounce up and down, which was peculiar in and of itself, as it seemed to be defying basic physics. After a few seconds, the movement got choppier, until finally it stopped, drifting almost horizontally in the air, pointing at the window. It seemed to float gently away from my sister, as if something were pulling at it. It was at once both mesmerizing and sinister. Gloria let out a muffled gasp, her hand flying up to cover her open mouth.

"Well, this is it," I uttered grimly. "This is where they're coming through."

—

The space where Nathan's missing screen had once been, became the opening of a kind of 'portal'. Disembodied entities don't travel through space in the same way that we do, because they aren't bound by the same physical laws of nature. It is not a difficult task for one or two of them to reach their geographical destination, however remote it might be, but when an interdimensional gateway is created, it allows for legions of wayward spirits to pour through. The more traffic it gets, the wider it becomes.

It is unclear to me why this particular portal opened, directly within the threshold of a 6-year-old's bedroom window, though it's similarly liminal nature may have played a part. One thing I do know, is that the more popular that portal becomes to the spirit realm, the more difficult it is to close. Regardless, I am happy to report that my sister and I did in fact close it that same day.

Gloria was extremely apologetic about the whole thing. Finances had been increasingly tough, due to the constant visits of technicians, trying to locate the electrical issue, and having to replace multiple electronics because of said issues. She couldn't offer us any monetary compensation for our service, but I assured her that there was no need. As I told her, if you're in this work purely for money, you're doing it for all the wrong reasons. This didn't quite seem to placate her, as she showed up at my house one evening, a few weeks later, carrying a box full of freshly baked loaves of bread for my family; her sweet, sincere way of showing her gratitude.

Since closing that portal, I've revisited their home, to get some bodywork from Gloria; a recently graduated Massage Therapist. She excitedly informed me that the family had done their 'homework', and followed my aftercare instructions to the letter. I confirmed this for myself, as my return visit felt as if I were in a completely different house altogether.

Nathan is sleeping in his own room again, and is no longer being dragged from his bed at night. The electrical issues ceased abruptly, and Gloria and Jeff have returned to the playful, loving couple that they had been before the phenomena began.

This was both one of my creepiest cases, and one of the most rewarding. It's not every day that one bears witness to such a potent gateway, nor is it common to meet a young child who is so consumed by negative energy that his gaze burns holes into the very core of your being. I am continually grateful that I was able to help that family out, and I wish them all the best in maintaining their healthy, happy home.

Phil Mendoza & Patricia K. Reyes

Case Study 7: The Juarez Family

The earthy blend of sage and patchouli drifted through the thin velvet curtain that separated my workspace from the rest of the shop, as I began gathering up my divination instruments. The steady chatter of potential customers had dissipated, and I was fairly certain that there wouldn't be much more business for the remainder of that Sunday evening.

Every weekend, I spent a few hours at the local occult shop, Gypsy Haven, offering my services and doing geomancy readings for their clientele. It was a great way to practice my craft, help people, and make a bit of extra cash in the process. Besides, the owner had become a good friend of mine over the years, and he sends quite a few clients my way.

"You taking off Phil?" he asked, straightening a stack of books on a nearby display.

"Yeah," I responded, switching off the small lamp on my makeshift desk. "Now that it's dark out, I doubt we'll get any more customers."

It was late in September, and the sun had begun setting earlier and earlier, which consequently meant less foot traffic the later into the evening it got. A glance at my phone confirmed that it was nearly 8 o'clock in the evening, and I still had quite a bit of my own work to do at home. After replenishing my stack of business cards on the front counter, I made my way towards the exit.

As I reached the door, a young woman with long, silky black hair and a worried look was entering the store. I nodded at her in greeting, allowing her to enter before taking my leave. I was shoving my duffel bag into my truck, when I heard my name being called from the direction of the shop.

"Phil!" the dark-haired young woman called out, sprinting towards my truck. "You're Phil, right?"

"I am," I answered, turning to face her. "What can I do for you?"

"The man behind the counter said you're the person to talk to about getting rid of evil spirits and things like that," she said, her voice tinged with anxiety. "Do you have a second to talk?"

"Absolutely," I assured her, gesturing for her to follow me. "Let's go sit down, and you can tell me all about it."

I led her back inside and into my little office, closing the curtain and hanging my 'Do Not Disturb' sign across the entrance. Over the course of the next hour, the young woman, who introduced herself as Marisol Juarez, relayed to me the story of what had been happening to her and her family for the last few years.

———

Marisol and her family had lived in a house by the lake for as long as she could remember. Her mother had passed away from cancer

76

when Marisol was still very young, and she remembered very little about her. She'd also had an older brother, who was killed in a severe car accident when Marisol was about 10 years old. Now, their family consisted of her father, Hector, and her two younger sisters, Esperanza and Rosa.

All her life, Marisol and her sisters had consistently experienced strange phenomena around their house; flickering lights, odd smells, shadow figures, and even the occasional apparition. Their father had brushed their claims aside, convinced that the overactive imagination of childhood was the real culprit. Besides, they were a devout Catholic household, and such claims had no place in their home.

Deeply frustrated by these occurrences, Marisol had planned to move out as soon as she turned 18. As if by divine intervention, she had happened upon what seemed like a perfect opportunity; a priest from a nearby parish offered to let her live in the top floor of the chapel, rent free, provided that she took care of the cleaning and upkeep of the church and the land surrounding it.

Marisol had immediately jumped at the offer; it was a great chance to get out and live on her own. Additionally, she'd been convinced that whatever was behind the paranormal phenomena at her family's home wouldn't dare to bother her in the house of God. By all accounts, it seemed like the perfect arrangement.

Her new position had begun uneventfully. The daily tasks required of her had been straightforward, and demanded very little time to complete. However, as the months went by, she'd begun feeling a low-level anxiety every time she was alone in the church. She'd noticed that, while dusting the sacristy one day, she couldn't shake the feeling of being watched.

Scanning the room, she'd confirmed that she was in fact alone. Still, that eerie feeling had remained. Over the days that followed, an unnamed fear had begun to grow inside her mind. Every time she was alone in the church, she'd had to fight the urge to run out; it felt as though she was being stalked by some invisible predator. That seemingly ideal living arrangement had begun to feel less and less like a blessing.

One evening, after she'd completed her chores for the day, she'd been relaxing up in her apartment. She'd been reading a book, curled up in bed, when her peace was disrupted by the sound of children's laughter, coming from the next room. Once the shock had worn off, she'd crept quietly into the living room, determined to catch the delinquents in the act. However, as soon as she'd rounded the corner, the laughter went silent, and no one was there.

Over the days that followed, the mysterious laughter had persisted. The visitations had increased, in both frequency and severity, and Marisol had quickly reached a point where she was convinced that she was losing her mind. Then, one fateful night, she'd witnessed something harrowing, that proved to her beyond a shadow of a doubt that something supernatural was indeed taking place in that church.

She'd been getting ready for bed, and had gone to turn off the overhead light in her living room, before heading to the bathroom to wash up. As she made her way to the light switch on the far wall, she'd caught sight of movement out of the corner of her eye. What she saw absolutely terrified her.

Before her were two young boys, dressed in what appeared to be funerary garb. They'd appeared to be about 8 years old, with ghostly pale skin and jet-black hair. They were skipping around the room gleefully, holding a black satin sash between the two of them.

Her initial reaction had been anger, as she'd been convinced that they'd wandered into her apartment from the chapel downstairs. In a huff of indignation, she'd yelled at them to leave; this was her personal living space and was off limits to members of the congregation.

One of the boys had ignored her orders, as if he hadn't heard her at all. The other boy had stopped what he was doing, and slowly swiveled his head in her direction. The corner of his mouth curled into a sneer, and he'd beamed back at her with a mischievous, sinister smile. Before she could even formulate a response, both boys turned, as if to leave, and vanished, leaving behind a pile of black ashes and that peculiar black satin sash.

Immediately, Marisol had burnt the only remnant of her encounter, and prayed fervently over the ashes. The memory of that otherworldly sash had haunted her dreams, threatening to unravel her sanity. Uncertain of how to handle what she was dealing with, she'd confronted the parish priest who'd offered her the position, and told him what she'd been experiencing.

It hadn't taken much convincing, and she'd been surprised at how readily he'd believed her. He'd squeezed her shoulder reassuringly and printed out some prayers for her to recite, in the event that the apparitions returned. This temporarily comforted her, and, armed with a renewed faith, she'd resumed her daily duties with confidence. Unfortunately, her reprieve was not meant to last.

A couple of days later, the boys returned. Quickly, she'd retrieved the prayers given to her by the priest, and recited them in earnest. At first, the prayers seemed to do the trick; the apparitions dissipated immediately, leaving her at peace once more. However, the effects of the prayers were short-lived. Although she'd succeeded in making the entities leave, they continued to reappear, and it became more and more difficult to get rid of them. She would also soon find that the incessant haunting was not relegated to her apartment.

Shortly before she'd moved out, her father had been diagnosed with Alzheimer's. He was still largely self-sufficient, though out of concern for his well-being, Marisol made it a point to stop by her childhood home as often as she could to check in on him. Her two younger sisters, Esperanza and Rosa, did as much as they could for him, between schoolwork and other household chores, but as the oldest, she felt it was her responsibility to take charge of the situation.

She'd fully expected that she'd have to navigate the effects of her father's memory lapses, especially in regards to basic daily tasks, such as paying bills or doing small repairs around the house. What she couldn't have predicted was that, perhaps for the first time in his life, her father had begun experiencing paranormal activity as well.

As the disease progressed, it appeared to have taken with it the veil of denial that her father had built up over his adult years, which had buffered him against the experiences that his daughters had so frequently reported. Seemingly out of nowhere, Hector Juarez had begun seeing movement in the shadows and strange orbs of light that he'd previously chalked up to the overactive imagination of his young daughters. Perhaps the most upsetting account of all, was that he'd been seeing two young boys, matching the precise description as the ones Marisol had been seeing in her apartment, skulking around their family's lake house.

He'd been seeing them almost nightly, peering in through the windows at him, and he could hear their laughter and footsteps from inside the house. Her father had even claimed that, sometimes, he would see them crawling out of the ground, from out of the base of the tree that they'd planted long ago, in honor of their brother who'd passed. Her once proud father had now been reduced to a blubbering mess, by eerie hauntings that, to him, were brand new.

Night after night, he'd insisted on leaving all the lights in the house on, terrified to be alone in the darkness. He would creep past the windows, tiptoeing quickly for fear of the ghost boys catching sight of him. He'd even begun refusing to sleep alone in his room, insisting that someone be nearby while he slept.

Even without supernatural interference, her father's diagnosis meant a very difficult road ahead. Most of Marisol's free time was occupied with running errands for her father, and making sure that his bills were all paid and up to date. The addition of the ghostly specters meant she was also frequently called out to help her sisters deal with their father's ever-worsening fears. The combination of all these things was almost too much to bear.

After a year of struggling to balance her time between tending to both her father and the church, and the nearly constant barrage of wicked supernatural visitations, Marisol finally decided to leave her post at the chapel and move back in with her family. The decision had been a difficult one to make, but she knew it was the right one.

When she'd informed Esperanza of her decision, and the underlying reason behind it, her sister had ridiculed her mercilessly. Rolling her eyes and sighing heavily, she'd told Marisol that there was no way anything evil was lurking in a house of God, and that she would gladly trade places with her. They discussed this with the parish priest, and made the switch a few days later.

Almost immediately, Esperanza began having the same experiences as her sister. Of course, she hadn't disclosed that fact until 6 months later, when she finally conceded her position. Sheepishly, she informed Marisol that she was right; something terrible was inhabiting that church, and she couldn't spend another night there.

Over a year after Marisol had originally moved out, Hector and his daughters were now back under the same roof; and now, they were all experiencing the paranormal activity as a family. Though the circumstances were not ideal, this newly found unity emboldened them, and Marisol had resolved to find a way to rid them of the apparitions for good.

—

Marisol's search had led her to where she was now, seated across the table from me, in a small alcove at Gypsy Haven. In the soft lamplight, her eyes appeared heavy with tears; or perhaps it was just sadness. Either way, I'd already decided to take her case.

The morning of my first visit was overcast and foggy; a fitting backdrop for the energy I was confronted with upon entering the home. Beneath that cloud of uncertainty was a family desperate and afraid, hoping and praying for peace, above all. And, although I could feel the oppressive energy clearly, there wasn't any concrete evidence to report. It took a multitude of visits, and subsequent banishings, over the course of the better half of a year, to finally free the Juarez family from the hold of darkness.

Although the ghostly boys had originally appeared at the church, the Juarez family was only concerned with cleansing their own home of the entities. They'd all resolved not to return to that particular congregation, and besides, I was not at all comfortable with doing any of my work in an established place of worship; that was the business of the Catholic authorities. My client was the Juarez family, not the local clergy.

It was extremely difficult to pinpoint the source of the oppression in this particular case. The phenomenon seemed to be occurring in two different locations, sometimes simultaneously, and there were no specific connections between the two that I could find; the only linking thread I was aware of was Marisol.

The land surrounding large bodies of water is home to a multitude of elemental and spiritual activity; along with its own biological ecosystem, such reservoirs are also known to be conductors, as they tend to amplify all manner of otherworldly energies. It was never fully clear to me if the phenomena from Marisol's childhood and the ghostly boys from the church were two separate manifestations, or if they were from similar sources. Certainly, the two streams interacted with and amplified one other, and it is indeed possible that the only connection between them was Marisol herself.

Not long after my work with the Juarez family had concluded, I discovered that the parish priest, who had originally offered Marisol the position, had been accused, and found guilty, of sexually assaulting a staggering amount of altar boys over the years. The abuse had been ritualistic in nature, which left no doubt in my mind that his actions were responsible for the ghostly boys who'd appeared to both Marisol and her father. Not only had his victims been physically violated, but they'd been invaded spiritually as well, through their unwilling participation in the priest's satanic practices.

A transgression that vile often creates a crack in our world, opening the space up to entities with malevolent intentions. It also leaves a scar on the psyche of its victims, sometimes splitting and mangling their spirit, culminating in such hauntings; they become echoes of the children they once were, now broken and emptied out. The priest's actions were unspeakable, and I desperately hope that the victims will find some sort of peace in the knowledge that he will now be held responsible for his crimes.

Phil Mendoza & Patricia K. Reyes

Case Study 8: Scott

C hunks of salt crunched beneath my work boots as I exited my kid's favorite pizza place, balancing a stack of hot, grease-stained cardboard boxes in one hand, and a 2-liter of Pepsi in the other. It was early evening, on a crisp Friday in late February, and I'd promised to bring dinner home with me. As I loaded everything into my truck, I noticed that I had a missed call, and subsequent voicemail, both from a number that was not in my contacts. I reasoned that it would be best to get dinner home before it got cold, and decided to check the voicemail then.

By the time I got home and handed off the food to the starving masses, I noticed that I'd also gotten a text message from the same number. In it, a person who introduced himself as Scott Jacobsen informed me that he was contacting me in reference to my 'spiritual' services. Making a mental note to call him back after I ate, I joined the feast already underway in the kitchen.

I'd promised my son and daughter that we'd watch a movie together that night, so it took some sweet-talking, and the possibility of getting ice cream that weekend, to get the time I needed to return Scott's call. Once I'd finally reached him, I was met with an unexpectedly jovial greeting.

"Hey man," came a good-natured, male voice. "I got your number through one of my bandmates; they know someone who knows you, or somethin' like that. They said you helped them out with some real weird shit going down in their house, so I figured you were the one to call."

"Well, you figured correctly," I responded with a chuckle. "What's up?"

Over the next 45 minutes or so, Scott relayed his story to me. As far as he could tell, the current phenomena had begun just over a year ago, after his two younger siblings, Ryan and Britney, had grown and moved out of their childhood home.

It had been roughly seven years since their father, Rick Jacobsen, passed away from lung cancer. A machinist by trade and a heavy smoker, Rick had been an incredibly belligerent man when he was alive. He'd taken every opportunity presented to him to abuse Scott's mother, Cynthia, and all three children, both verbally and physically. After a year of battling cancer, having undergone both chemotherapy and radiation treatments, the disease took its toll and Rick gave up the ghost. While the family had mourned his passing, there was also an unspoken sigh of relief; they were finally free of their abuser.

Over the years that followed, the remaining Jacobsen family had picked up the pieces of their broken home, and eventually thrived without Rick around. Though Scott, the eldest of the children, had long-since moved out, he visited frequently, to check in on his family and to take advantage of the veritable recording studio that he had constructed in the basement over the years. His music had always been his outlet, even before his father passed, and it was most certainly where he devoted most of his time.

Once Ryan and Britney had moved out, Cynthia decided that it was finally the appropriate time in her life to start getting out and dating again. After a few misfires, she'd found a kind, retired older man, who became increasingly devoted to caring for her. However, in the midst of her newfound happiness, she'd begun to notice strange things happening around the house.

The first sign of supernatural interference had been the smell of cigarettes, that seemed to follow her around the house. This had been particularly upsetting, because the scent was identical to the cigarettes that her late husband had smoked. It had been just subtle enough to be unnerving; she'd almost expected to look up and see Rick coming towards her, his fists clenched and his face twisted in rage.

As if that weren't unsettling enough, she'd begun to see shadows moving through the house. Frequently, she'd get the profound sense that her late husband's anger, a thick, palpable energy, hung heavily in the air around her. It had felt as though Rick was still present somehow, in the form of a jilted spirit, vengeful that his wife had had the audacity to move on with her life.

Initially, Scott had written this off as some subconscious sense of guilt that his mother had been clinging to about re-entering the dating pool. Or, he thought, perhaps years of abuse had trained her to expect Rick's wrath at every turn, making it difficult to accept something good coming into her life. Either way, Scott hadn't been especially concerned at that point.

Shortly after his mother had begun reporting the phenomena, Scott and his bandmates had met up at his childhood home to practice some songs they were working on. Before that, Scott had not experienced anything out of the ordinary happen around the house, and he wasn't about to let his mother's irrational fears keep him from working on his music.

The band had run through one of their songs a few times, and were busy exchanging notes about what could be done differently and what they needed to work on, when his drummer's coffee mug had flown across the room, shattering against the far wall. A stunned silence had fallen over the group, as they glanced around, trying to figure out what had just happened. Then, before any of them had had a chance to speak, a stack of guitar picks started flying off a nearby shelf, zipping past Scott's head. That was when it had hit him: the distinct scent of cigarette smoke.

For a moment, Scott had been rendered speechless, flashing back to a vision of his enraged father, furious about the loud music, and he'd felt the instinctual urge to flinch, as if he'd fully expected the familiar sensation of his father's fist slamming against his face. He must have blanched out of fear, because by the time he'd regained his composure, the entire band was staring at him; both unnerved by the phenomena and concerned for their friend.

Going forward, Scott had treated his mother's fears with considerably more gravity. Having witnessed the bizarre events firsthand, he was becoming increasingly concerned for his mother's safety, and made it a point to check in on her daily, even if it was just a phone call. Unfortunately, his worst fears would soon be realized.

Early one evening, he'd received a call from Emergency Services, informing him that his mother was being rushed to the hospital. She'd fallen down the stairs in the house, striking her head in the process. That blow had triggered a stroke, which had taken with it her motor skills, paralyzing the entire right side of her body. Once she was in stable condition, and her children were at her side, she'd proceeded to tell them what had happened.

She'd been getting ready for bed, after an early dinner with the man she'd been seeing. As she made her way towards the top of the stairs, she'd felt two large hands grasp her by the shoulders, gripping them tightly. She'd paused for a moment, and was quickly overwhelmed by the formidable scent of tobacco. Then, in a split second that felt like hours, she'd felt the invisible hands violently shove her forward, sending her careening down the stairs. Thankfully, she'd had her cellphone in her pocket, which somehow remained undamaged from the fall, and she'd been able to dial 9-1-1 from where she landed.

Cynthia had been in her early 60's at the time, and had never had a single health problem; other than injuries related to her husband's abuse, of course. There had been no reason to suspect any sort of dementia or seizure was at play in her accident. Even so, her doctor had run a handful of tests, just to be certain, all of which had come back negative. Nothing physiological or neurological had been at play in her fall.

Scott's mother had remained in the hospital for a month and a half, and then spent another month at a live-in rehabilitation facility. She, very literally, had to learn how to walk again, and at the time of my conversation with Scott, she had yet to achieve full mobility on her right side.

Understandably, Scott was deeply concerned for his mother's safety. He'd almost lost her that fateful night, and she deserved to finally have some peace and happiness in her life. Both him and his mother suspected that it was the late Rick Jacobsen, still hanging around and tormenting them, furious at being swept aside and forgotten, but they couldn't be sure. All they knew was that it needed to stop as soon as possible.

After I'd jotted down my notes, I got the address for his mother's house, and we arranged a time for me to come out and do a walkthrough. I scribbled a reminder to do my divinations before the visit onto a sticky note, and rejoined my children for movie night.

———

It was a sunny Saturday morning in early March, when I pulled into Cynthia Jacobsen's driveway. The home, a sprawling tri-level structure, sat on the corner of a sleepy, suburban neighborhood, with large windows facing the street, surrounded by massive oak trees. It was unseasonably warm, and I decided to leave my jacket in the truck, before making my way to the front door.

Before I could ring the doorbell, the door swung open, and I was greeted by a man in his early 40's, donning socks, tattered denim jeans, and a faded blue t-shirt. He met me with a huge grin and reached to shake my hand.

"You're Scott, I take it," I offered, meeting him with a firm handshake.

"That's my name," he laughed. "Or, so they tell me!"

After stepping inside, I removed my boots, to avoid tracking debris into their home. Scott's mother was away at physical therapy for the day, and we had the place to ourselves. The entryway was spacious, as was the rest of the house. With two separate living areas, a massive kitchen, and three floors to work with, it would have been an ideal house in which to raise a big family. The larger living room had a huge skylight, which bathed most of the space in sunlight, and it was where we finally sat down to talk after viewing the entirety of the home.

My investigation was largely inconclusive, in terms of any objective, qualitative information. I also hadn't had quite the same initial trepidation at entering the home that I'd had in some of my previous cases. However, there was a distinct sense of oppression that permeated the property, that was very difficult to shake.

It felt like being slowly suffocated, and the air felt stagnant and bloated, heavy with a nameless rage. This wasn't immediately noticeable, but as my visit progressed, it became harder and harder to breathe. It was as if all the oxygen had been sucked out of the room as we sat down on the sofa. I relayed this all to Scott, and he nodded knowingly in response.

"Now that you mention it, that's how it felt every time dad was home," he muttered quietly, his countenance becoming that of scared child. "Is it him?"

I took a moment to formulate my answer. I needed to be as truthful as possible in giving him my answer, while also being considerate of his trauma. This entire family had been through a lot, and the last thing I wanted to do was reinforce their fear of this larger-than-life image of their deceased patriarch; I didn't want to allow him any more of that power.

"I believe that it may very well be, but I need you to understand something," I started, choosing my words carefully. "Whatever is behind these incidents, even if it is your father, has no right to be here. Your fear of him gives the phenomena strength; even if it's not actually his spirit at work here."

Scott nodded numbly, without meeting my gaze.

"The dead need to move on, to whatever awaits them," I continued with caution. "With your permission, I'd like to begin cleansing the space and banishing whatever is oppressing this house."

Finally, Scott turned to look back at me, a look of resolve in his eyes.

"Do whatever you have to do. I want Mom to feel safe again."

Without another word, I began unpacking my tools and set up the area to do my banishing ritual. Scott took his leave, making his way towards the backyard, where he was going to wait until I'd finished. The tension in the air began to thicken palpably, as I set the intentions for the work I was about to do. With candles lit and the scent of incense filling my nostrils, I started reciting my prayers.

The air felt dense, and for some reason it seemed to burn in my lungs. As I began casting my circle, there was a peculiar quiver in the energy of the room; a low vibration, as if something was preparing to manifest. Just as I began to evoke the entity oppressing the house, a figure materialized, right at the edge of my protective barrier; fully visible and clearly enraged.

"I HAVE A RIGHT TO BE HERE," the specter growled. Its features were blurred, as if they'd been drawn in ink and then smudged. It looked vaguely like the photos I'd seen of Rick Jacobsen, but it seemed somehow slighter, and hunched over a bit. What would have been flesh, if it were still human, was covered in red splotches, that resembled a rash or a chemical burn. Instantly, the smell of cigarette smoke enveloped me. This was definitely the thing that was haunting the Jacobsen family home.

"THIS IS *MY* HOUSE," came the rasping voice again. "THIS IS *MY* FAMILY."

I ignored its protests, knowing that little good ever came from engaging with an entity you were trying to remove. Fervently, I continued on with my incantations, desperately fighting the urge to cough; it felt like my lungs were filling up with fiberglass.

It took the better part of two hours to complete my work. The husk that had once been Rick Jacobsen had been banished; at least for now. It tugged at the back of my mind, and I did a quick divination to confirm my suspicions. Finally, I packed up my tools, and went to retrieve Scott from the backyard and inform him of my findings.

The culprit was gone for now, and its hold had been severely weakened. However, I would need to return a few more times, to ensure that the spirit was fully removed from the home and had moved on for good.

As I explained all of this to Scott, his posture shrank, almost imperceptibly. I could feel both his grief and his guilt, permeating his aura. Both his love for his father and his hatred of how he'd treated Scott and the rest of his family weighed heavily on him. Reconciling those emotions was sure to be a lengthy and difficult journey, and I empathized deeply with him. My work with the Jacobsen family was reaching an end, but I sensed that their healing was just beginning.

———

During my final visit to the Jacobsen home, I was reminded of the odd appearance that Rick's apparition had taken. We sat down to a cup of coffee before I took my leave, and I described what I'd seen to Scott and his mother. A look of recognition passed over their faces, and they proceeded to explain why the spirit had manifested in such a way.

Towards the end of his life, Rick's torso had been covered in dark red welts, which had been caused by radiation burns from the treatments he'd undergone. That final, traumatizing memory had remained with his spirit, and he'd appeared to me in the last way that he remembered himself. This was an especially intriguing element of this case, as it speaks to the nature of disembodied spirits.

How much of who we were remains, after our body expires? And, how is that determined? This was unlike anything I'd witnessed before, in my years of doing this sort of work, and the memory of that visage is still very much alive in my mind.

Another significant aspect of this particular cluster of phenomena, was the symbolism of Cynthia being paralyzed on her right side after her harrowing accident. In metaphysical terms, the right side of the human body is associated with the masculine, the left with the feminine. To extrapolate this a bit further, the archetype of masculinity is active, associated with movement and power, while the archetypal feminine is passive, associated with stillness and receptivity. So, when the spirit that was once Rick pushed Cynthia down the stairs, resulting in paralysis of her entire right side, he was symbolically taking away her power; her power to move on and live her own life. This was certainly in line with how he treated his wife when he was still alive.

Lastly, the span of time between Rick's death and his reappearance as a malevolent entity in their home was substantial. It definitely brings up a variety of questions regarding where the soul goes when it passes over, and how long it can remain there. Where was Rick's energy for that seven-year span of time? Does time have any meaning on that plane of existence?

Similarly, what is it that draws a spirit back to its old home? Was it a sense of familiarity, or simply his memory that still remained in the minds of those left behind? It is extremely unusual, in my experience, to have such a great time lapse between a person's death and any subsequent hauntings they might have a hand in. Had I not had such overwhelming evidence, including very clear confirmation from my divination, I would have ruled out the possibility that it was in fact Rick Jacobsen's ghost oppressing that house.

The Jacobsen family home remains undisturbed to this day. Cynthia has found a loving companion with which to live out her twilight years, and Scott and his band are still making music. I am grateful to have been able to help initiate their healing process, and I am confident that they will continue to grow and thrive in the future.

Case Study 9: John

Raindrops glistened on the leaves of an aging oak tree in my backyard, and the scent of earth engulfed my senses, as I reverently sipped my tea. It was a cool Saturday afternoon in May, as I sat on my back porch, silently relishing the sounds and smells of nature. A pair of doves cooed softly from my fence, where they often perched, and eyed me curiously.

I'd just received a call from a new potential client, whose claims were almost too extraordinary to be believed. My gut instinct was that he was being truthful, but I was having trouble wrapping my mind around the possibilities his report implied. I didn't want to believe him; the alleged phenomena were far too disruptive to my current perspective on reality. However, I'd followed up our conversation with a round of preliminary divinations, all of which had confirmed the validity of this client's story, and I'd decided to take a break and ponder what he'd relayed to me.

As I sat there, meditating quietly, a flash of light caught my eye. A tiny glass prism, which my daughter had hung from a tree branch, spun back and forth lazily in the breeze, catching the rays of the sun. The refracted light beamed onto the ground, into the form of a pale rainbow, bouncing around on the concrete. I watched it dance, back and forth, and considered its source.

Where did that ephemeral rainbow come from? Was it a product of rudimentary human senses, compiling their best guess from the resources it had available? Was it simply the light of the sun? Or some property of the prism itself? The answer, of course, was all of the above. It was a wholly unique, emergent phenomenon, with a valid, though illusory, existence. This was the precise nature of the case upon which I was about to embark.

John Matthis was a military counselor, who treated veterans with Post Traumatic Stress Disorder (PTSD). Most, if not all, of his clients, had seen combat, in many of the most remote areas of the globe, and they would come to him for help in processing these terrifying, brutal experiences. Having been in the service himself, John had a deep empathy for his clients, and a firsthand understanding of the hardships they endured after being discharged.

In the early days of his counseling career, John had been conducting all of his sessions out of his home; a sprawling, 5-bedroom cabin, located deep in the mountains of northern California, near Mt. Shasta. The location was remote, and as such he felt it was the ideal place for his clients to work through their trauma and heal. He himself had always had a deep love for nature, and preferred to be in the presence of trees and wildlife. As he'd spent years processing his own traumatic experiences from his time in combat, he'd found the location to be extremely conducive to his own inner work. Initially, he'd been correct, and his practice had been wildly successful, which made the ensuing strangeness all the more perplexing.

When he'd first begun hearing voices and seeing shadow figures moving about his property, his default assumption was that it was just stress. John's mind was already scarred by his own wartime conflicts, but as he listened to more and more of his clients' stories, the weight of it all was overwhelming. Combat veterans are often privy to more than their fair share of violence and gore, but also to a plethora of unexplained phenomena that they are warned not to talk about.

It is a fact of daily life for many service members, though they are told on no uncertain terms to keep it to themselves, at the risk of being labelled disturbed, and unfit for duty. The western incursion into the Middle East and other more remote areas of the globe constantly opens up a new realm of beliefs and practices to American soldiers, who are ill-equipped to deal with what they were experiencing. Upon being discharged, they are thrown back into society, with little means or opportunity to reassimilate successfully. Few of them return the same person they were before they were deployed. That was where John's work began.

Over time, his practice had grown. He'd helped many veterans overcome their trauma and reintegrate into society; unfortunately, some clients were still lost to suicide. This was not uncommon in the population that he worked with, but that did not cushion the emotional blows he took when he lost a patient. Still, he believed that the work he was doing was important, and he was sincerely dedicated to continuing it; even though he was beginning to suspect it was taking a toll on his sanity.

Eventually, it was as if an energetic tipping point had been reached. The noises he'd been hearing previously, now occurred at all hours of the night. He often awoke to the sounds of crying or screaming from somewhere outside, coming from the direction of the forest. He'd hear voices, which sounded like they were right outside his bedroom window. They were incoherent, but palpable; as if a group of people had gathered in the woods outside, having a conversation, in a language he didn't understand.

As the weeks crept by, John became more and more convinced that his grip on reality was loosening. The indiscernible voices, mysterious shadows, and blood-curdling screams were a nightly occurrence, and sleep began to elude him. In that liminal space between dreams and awakening, the dark figures began taking on defined features in his mind, whispering secrets that he would forget the next morning. During the day, his property seemed to come alive with wildlife, as if all the local fauna had been personally invited.

Frequent sightings of deer, rabbits, and other forest-dwelling creatures became commonplace for him. In the twilight hours of the evenings, there would be constant movement from the tree line, accompanied by the distinct sense of being watched. He'd once considered installing cameras around the perimeter of his home, but had decided against it, in the interest of protecting the confidentiality of his clients.

The phenomena continued to escalate, and, no matter how he tried to block it out or reason it all away, the sounds and sightings would not relent. The disturbances were reaching a fever pitch, until one night, he awoke to find himself lying in the middle of the woods, with no idea where he was or how he'd gotten there. This quickly became a regular occurrence, and there seemed to be little he could do to prevent it. The following is an account of one such evening, as John has relayed it to me.

———

John woke with a start, shivering against the biting chill in the atmosphere. With a dissatisfied grunt, he reached out to pull the duvet up around his shoulders, groping clumsily at the empty space next to him. Instead of finding his faithful old comforter, his hand grasped at what felt like twigs and clumps of dirt. Confused, he sat up, rubbing the sleep from his eyes and looking around.

His heart skipped a beat, as he found himself sprawled out between massive redwood trees and dense shrubbery. The full moon beamed overhead, illuminating the unfamiliar space he found himself in. Beyond the slight clearing, everything was enveloped in the deep velvet darkness.

How the hell had he gotten out here? Was it just a particularly vivid dream? He pinched his thigh sharply, only to discover that he was indeed fully lucid.

For a moment he sat there, trying desperately to recall the last thing he remembered before falling asleep that night. He had no history of sleepwalking, but it was the only logical explanation for his predicament. With no neighbors for miles, he couldn't imagine it had been some kind of sick practical joke. Feeling around in the pale moonlight, he couldn't find any injuries on his person, or any evidence of needle marks or restraints. He was still in the faded plaid boxer shorts and threadbare undershirt that he'd been wearing when he crawled into bed. That was when he noticed the silence.

Although he appeared to be deep in the woods, the clearing was completely quiet. Even at night, the forest should be teeming with wildlife. At the very least, he should have heard the rustling of branches, or movements in the bushes, as the forest's nocturnal inhabitants went about their business. Yet, he could hear nothing but his heartbeat, pounding in his ears.

Out of the corner of his eye, he spotted movement from behind an especially towering pine tree. Immediately, he leapt to his feet, turning to face whatever was coming for him. He wasn't entirely sure what he'd expected to see, but nothing could have prepared him for what presented itself.

From behind the massive trunk, a chunky white rabbit hopped out, eyeing him brazenly. Confidently, and without a trace of hesitation, it bounced towards him, its blanched fur making it look almost translucent in the moonlight. Cautiously, John squatted down to get a better look at his furry visitor.

For the briefest of moments, the pair sat there, eyeing each other in some sort of surreal standoff. The rabbit's nose twitched back and forth, and its eyes glowed with an otherworldly red aura. As John sat there entranced, images kept flowing into his mind: a dusty desert landscape littered with mountains of corpses; a black, smoky cloud, pulsing and expanding; thick, crimson liquid, staining the pure white of freshly fallen snow; a billowing spray of burnt orange, rolling through a jungle, as if the air itself was on fire; children in stretchers, their features deformed and grotesque, weeping in pain and confusion.

Assaulted with the weight of these images, John fell back sharply onto his backside, loosening his focus on the odd creature before him. A high-pitched ringing pierced his eardrums, and he fell forward, palms plunging into the moist earth beneath him. His body shuddered in protest against the invisible force of gravity that seemed to keep him pinned in place.

Suddenly, the rabbit's tiny form began to grow and shift. Its spine lengthened and expanded, and thick black fur began to grow over its once stark white coat. The ears shrank and reformed, sticking straight up into dark triangular points, and its skull twisted and narrowed, into a long snout. In the span of seconds, the white rabbit before him had transformed into an impossibly massive black wolf, whose eyes shone with the same reddish glow as its previous form.

By now, John was fully convinced that he was experiencing a complete mental breakdown. This thing before him simply could not exist. It could not be real. Then, in an act that further divorced the creature from reality, it began to speak.

In the shadows, it seemed as though its jaw were moving in time with the cadence of its speech, even though John was fully aware that it was in no way physically possible for an animal to do so. It was a language that he'd never heard before, but it felt as if it were pressing into his mind, and somehow, he understood it. However, no matter how hard he tried to keep the words in his mind, to commit them to memory, they slipped away, like some cryptic message in a dream. After what simultaneously felt like an eternity and the blink of an eye, the creature shifted forms one final time.

The dark, looming shape of the wolf began to shrink and fade, becoming a thick, translucent mist, and eventually it stood up on its hind legs, to become a tall, humanoid figure. There were no defining features to speak of, aside from its upright, four-limbed posture; it was like looking at an image in a video game, that hadn't fully resolved. It didn't look particularly threatening, other than its impossible ability to shapeshift, but it didn't exactly feel welcoming either.

What felt like hours passed, and he never once took his eyes off the humanoid figure. Images kept pouring into his mind, accompanied by strange phrases and sensations. He had no way of gauging how long they remained like that, locked into that dreamlike, ethereal communion.

The next thing John remembered was waking up in the dirt once more; though this time, the sun was coming up, and his mythical visitor was nowhere to be seen. Exhausted, and with holes in his socks, he was eventually able to find his way back to the main road. Following it back to his home, he was shocked to find that his front door was unlocked, and there was no evidence of foul play to be found.

—

Even for me, and the multitude of bizarre accounts I've heard while doing this work, John's story was absolutely unbelievable. His experiences breached the boundaries of what, up until this point, I'd believed was possible. When I sat down to do my divinations about this case, I fully expected to be shown that his stories were pure fantasy, or that he'd simply had a mental breakdown. However, that is not what happened. No matter how many different ways I could surmise to rephrase my questions, the response always came back the same: he was telling me the truth, and these events were indeed taking place.

At the time I met John, I was in the midst of a cluster of military-related cases; in my line of work, I'll often get a string of cases that have a specific theme, yet are unrelated to one another. A few months prior to our initial conversation, he'd moved out to Illinois to live with his aging mother. He'd believed that once he left his home in California behind, he'd be free of the otherworldly influences that had been tormenting him, as he had come to think that whatever was happening was related to the land his house had been built on. Unfortunately, these beings followed him halfway across the country, and he was still being plagued by the same voices and shadow figures as before.

Before doing any work in person, John and I had spent hours on the phone, and I'd filled the better half of a notebook with his accounts. My divinations regarding his phenomena were many and varied. Pinpointing the source of the phenomena was nearly impossible, as it became clear that what was happening to him was a conflagration of multiple threads, which had become entangled, and emerged as an entirely independent force.

As we've seen, severe trauma, such as military combat, fractures a person's mind and spirit, creating a space which many entities will attempt to occupy. If you combine John's personal trauma, with that of his clients', relived moment by moment during the course of their therapy sessions, a merging of currents takes place, forming a monstrous egregore of malevolent energy. That, coupled with the naturally potent elemental energy that is heavily present in the forests and land surrounding Mt. Shasta, culminated in the emergent phenomena that John was experiencing.

When it came time to actually perform the ritual work to rid John of his spiritual afflictions, I drove out to his mother's farmhouse in the rural, Illinois countryside. A mountain of a man, John was roughly 6-1/2 feet tall, well over 300 pounds, and in phenomenal shape. I'd just closed a case in which I was viciously assaulted by a man half John's size, who'd been overtaken by the oppressing entity. This had made me understandably nervous about doing our work in person. With a set of iron shackles heavy in my hands, I explained my concerns, and he agreed to being restrained while I did my banishing.

We were both pleasantly surprised to find that the restraints were wholly unnecessary. Although it took a handful of sessions to fully sever the ties that bound the phenomena to John, he was never once overtaken by any of those entities, and he never once got violent or aggressive the entire time I worked with him.

John checks in with me regularly, and to this day, he is doing well and his practice is thriving. He now has the tools to keep his sphere of sensation clean and his space free of spiritual parasites. I feel blessed, and humbled, to have had this opportunity to expand the boundaries of my own beliefs, and this still remains, by far, the strangest case of my career.

Epilogue

The ways in which a spiritual entity can manifest in one's life are many and varied. The most potent gateways to spiritual oppression are trauma, abuse, and addiction. The depth of these wounds on the human psyche has a way of fracturing one's spirit, leaving the person vulnerable to all manner of unseen influences; none of which have the person's best interest at heart.

Wayward spirits can see these wounds, like scars on your sphere of sensation. They can read your energy and see your trauma. They survey all of your baggage, your gifts, and your struggles; even the remnants of other entities that might have latched onto you in the past are visible to them. On the ethereal plane, there are no secrets.

The advice that I offer you, in order to avoid attracting any otherworldly parasites, is the same advice that I give to all of my clients. Find your faith. Figure out what you believe in, whatever that path might be, and live your life accordingly. Truly embodying your spiritual beliefs leaves little room for negative external influences in your life.

Similarly, practicing balance and moderation on a daily basis makes you a very challenging target for lower energies.

Imbalance in one's words or actions is, in a sense, giving away one's power. Whether it be alcohol, drugs, food, or sex, when we place an inordinate amount of focus on any one thing, we are demonstrating a lack of autonomy in our lives. This is a beacon for any starving entities that would gladly fill that power vacuum, who are desperate for the pain and exhilaration of being alive.

The purpose of this body of work is not to evoke fear in the heart of the reader. The purpose of this book is to create awareness about an ever-present threat to our quality of life. These things are very real, and not something to be taken lightly, or as a source of entertainment or pageantry. Any penetrating into the spirit realm is a two-way mirror; you can reach out to them, and they can just as easily reach back to grab you.

So, keep your sphere of sensation clean, and always maintain mindfulness and agency in your own life. Remain self-aware, yet unafraid to face your own personal demons. In so doing, not only will you strengthen your own spiritual sovereignty, but you will live a life of thriving and fulfillment in the process, becoming a more self-possessed and actualized individual.

Phil Mendoza & Patricia K. Reyes

About the Authors

Phil Mendoza was born and raised in the Chicagoland area, where he currently resides with his son and daughter. He has been a devoted student of the occult sciences for well over 25 years, and has enjoyed membership with a variety of esoteric orders. Currently, he does both geomancy readings and past life regressions for his blossoming client base in his precious spare time. He is a contributing member and an active adept in his local Golden Dawn Collegium, where he met his friend and co-author of his first book, Patricia K. Reyes. To connect with Phil, you can email him at: pmendoza7777@gmail.com

Patricia K. Reyes is a lifelong poet and student of the paranormal, who spent her formative years in the Central Valley of California. A master of spontaneous life decisions, she now resides in southeastern Michigan, with two demanding fur babies and one reptilian overlord. In her coveted spare time, she is a devoted occultist, an incorrigible psychonaut, and she dabbles in UFOlogy, existential philosophy, video games, and causing glitches in the simulation. Visit PatriciaKReyes.com for more.

Phil Mendoza & Patricia K. Reyes

They Devour in Silence

www.ingramcontent.com/pod-product-compliance
Lightning Source LLC
LaVergne TN
LVHW052032080426
835513LV00018B/2281

9798218197452